Richard Green

The Mission of Methodism

Richard Green

The Mission of Methodism

ISBN/EAN: 9783743332065

Manufactured in Europe, USA, Canada, Australia, Japa

Cover: Foto ©ninafisch / pixelio.de

Manufactured and distributed by brebook publishing software (www.brebook.com)

Richard Green

The Mission of Methodism

THE MISSION OF METHODISM

BEING THE

TWENTIETH FERNLEY LECTURE

DELIVERED IN BRISTOL, AUGUST 4TH, 1890

BY

THE REVEREND RICHARD GREEN

LONDON
WESLEYAN METHODIST BOOK-ROOM
2, CASTLE STREET, CITY ROAD, E.C.
AND 66, PATERNOSTER ROW, E.C.
1890

TO THE REVEREND

WILLIAM FIDDIAN MOULTON, M.A., D.D.

PRESIDENT

OF THE

WESLEYAN METHODIST CONFERENCE

THIS LECTURE

IS

AFFECTIONATELY INSCRIBED

SYNOPSIS OF LECTURE.

INTRODUCTION .   PAGE vii

CHAPTER I.

THE ESSENTIAL CHARACTERISTICS OF METHODISM AS ILLUSTRATED IN WESLEY'S PERSONAL HISTORY.

FOUR ELEMENTS :—

1. Conversion—Justification by Faith—Assurance . . 1
2. Elevation of Idea of the Christian Life—Entire Sanctification 21
3. Evangelism 28
4. Fellowship — The Society — Care for the Individual Believer—Employment of Gifts of Entire Church . 40

CHAPTER II.

THE MISSION OF METHODISM DEFINED.

1. Development of the Idea of Methodism in the Mind of Wesley   61

   EPOCHS :—

   (1) From 1738 to 1744.—Outburst of Evangelistic Spirit—No Plan—No Conference—Methodism Forming   62

   (2) From 1744 to 1749.—First Conferences—Doctrinal and Disciplinary Minutes—Progress of Definition—Consolidation 69

(3) Subsequent Development — Fourteen Years' Continuous Labour—No Annual Printed Minutes—Expansion—"Large Minutes"—Wesley's Precise Definition of the Calling of Methodism . . 86

2. Further Historical Development . . . 94

(1) Its Effective Vindication of the Truth—Mysticism—"Stillness"—Calvinism—Antinomianism . 94

(2) The Revival of the Religious Spirit in Church and Dissent — Influence on National Manners and Morals—Testimonies . . . 103

(3) Foreign Missions—English-Speaking Populations—Colonial Methodism 111

CHAPTER III.

HOW FAR HAS METHODISM HITHERTO BEEN FAITHFUL TO THE ESSENTIAL IDEA OF ITS MISSION?

Wesley's Purpose Bold—Adaptation of Methods—Test of Fidelity—First Successors to Wesley — Second Period — Changed Conditions—Sections of Methodism—Attitude To-day . 124

CHAPTER IV.

RELATION OF METHODISM TO THE FUTURE.

Has Methodism still a Mission? If so, what? . . 164

CONCLUSION . . 215

APPENDIX . 219

INTRODUCTION.

When the Board of Management did me the honour to ask me to deliver the Fernley Lecture, a desire was expressed that this year it should have a direct relation to Methodism; and when "The Mission of Methodism" was suggested to me as an appropriate subject, I saw at least a fitness in such a topic being treated in the city where we are now assembled, in which so many of the distinctive features of Methodism had their origin. It was in this city that the first Methodist meeting-house was erected; it was here that the first idea of the Methodist class-meeting, "the Bristol plan," was conceived; here the great departure, the field-preaching, was first made, by one whose name is ever to be honoured amongst us—George Whitefield. I am moreover reminded that it is just a hundred years since Mr. Wesley in this city presided at the last Conference he was permitted to attend; that this is the first year of the fourth jubilee of the founding of Methodism, and that in the course of next year the second Œcumenical Methodist Conference will be held, and this time in the country where Methodism has attained its greatest magnitude and achieved some of its grandest triumphs. In view of this important gathering, I feel that an additional interest attaches to my subject.

Methodism stands forth a fact in this age. Its history and its service are universally known. Its efficiency is neither dependent upon recognition being given, nor impaired by its being withheld. But we may ask ourselves, What is its place in the world to-day? What is its adaptation to the world's need? What is its calling—its mission? These questions we ask not with a view to justify the work of Methodism, but to illustrate it; we ask them partly for our satisfaction, partly for our guidance. It is permitted to us to stand and take our outlook over the world, the interest of whose history becomes daily more and more thrilling, and to endeavour to ascertain how far and in what way our appliances are capable of rendering service to it. We may not find much to amend, we may not find much to congratulate ourselves upon: but a glimpse of unfulfilled duty, of unoccupied ground, of greater possibilities, may stimulate to new and enlarged effort. Methodism needs no vindication at our hands: its history is its own best vindication. But if there be not a call for justification, there may be the highest advantage in trying, from an examination of its past history and of its adaptation to present requirements, to form a just judgment on its calling in the future. What Methodism is *able* to do may indicate what Methodism is *called* to do.

THE MISSION OF METHODISM.

CHAPTER I.

ESSENTIAL CHARACTERISTICS.

1. *Conversion.*

It has become a favourite method with modern writers to trace the current of a nation's history by the aid of the lives of workers in that history; as with others, to interpret the writings of an individual in the light of his life. It would be impossible to get to understand the process of the Reformation of the sixteenth century by an examination of the English Book of Common Prayer, or without the lives of Luther, Cranmer, and Melancthon, of Calvin, Erasmus, and Ulric Zwingle, of John Tetzel and Leo the Tenth. The upheavings of Italy, which issued in the formation of that great kingdom, would be inexplicable apart from the memoirs of Mazzini and Cavour, of Garibaldi and King Victor Emmanuel. And any great moral revolution must be estimated in view of the lives of its authors, by their surroundings, their aims and aspirations, as well as by the conditions of life and thought at the time within the religious sphere and around it. So is it here. The great change wrought in the condition of English life and morals, and in the great Church life of the English-speaking populations of the world during the last and present centuries, receives its brightest illumination from the lives and activities of a few honoured men, whose work underlay the great modern revival.

The history of the founding of Methodism is the history of the life of John Wesley, and of his little band of fellow-workers; but pre-eminently it is found in the life of Wesley himself. If I give prominence to John Wesley, it is only as a representative. Although, as I have said, the entire work finds its most complete embodiment in him, Whitefield, Charles Wesley, and afterwards Fletcher and others are always within my view when I speak of their great leader. The honour of the work, as was the labour, is to be shared by all. They together formed the centre around which the elements of Methodism gathered.

But from the beginning to the end of his career he was its leader and master-spirit. Everything within it bore the stamp of his hand, and, if not created by him, was moulded by his skill. He kept guard over it, defended and controlled it. He directed its activities; he selected its agents. Nothing was admitted into its organization without his permission. The entire genius of Methodism was embodied in him. It cannot be studied but by the aid of his life. It would be unwise to enter upon an examination of the religious system without first studying the religious reformer. He who would understand the system must be familiar with the man. Methodism was essentially Wesleyan. The terms are almost convertible.

I shall be guided by this fact, and seek to trace the essential characteristics of Methodism as they are illustrated in Wesley's personal history. This must be my apology, if one is needed, for treating my subject to so large an extent historically.

Were this subject pursued to its utmost limits, it would be necessary to pay some regard to the quiet work of preparation which affected Wesley's own character, and to those external conditions which helped so much to determine his course; to have respect to all that relates to his interesting ancestry, to his early discipline, to the character of English society into which he was born, and amidst which he moved. The state of religious thought and the condition of the English Churches would come fairly within the scope of this part of the inquiry.

It would be difficult to mark any distinct moment when it could be said that Methodism began, so gradual was the development. Many unseen causes contributed to prepare the way for a work, the demand for which had become so intense as to have reached a critical stage. The purpose of the Divine Providence to meet the spiritual necessities of the time must be seen to have been working, hidden as a seed in the ground, long before it appeared in the actual preparation of the agents designed for its accomplishment.

Passing over years of great interest, for the story of which it is sufficient that I refer to the many "Lives" of Wesley that have issued from the press, let our attention be first given to him when he was in his early undergraduate years, before any settled purpose in life had seized him, when his mind was open to the many influences that were playing around him, but which had so far failed to exert any controlling power over him. He was careful in the ordering of his time, was diligent in study, said his prayers both in public and private, and read the Scriptures and several books of religion, especially Comments on the New Testament, and he attended the Holy Communion, as he was bound to do, three times in the year.

At the same time he tells us that he went on habitually, and for the most part contentedly, in some known sin or other—a very indefinite statement when we remember what were his views of sin at the time he penned it. But the grasp of his father's hand was upon him, and the gentle breath of his mother's voice swayed him.

He could not be insensible to these even in Oxford. He had been too carefully tutored for his conscience to lose its authority without a great decay of moral sentiment and some flagrant departure into evil. When he was twenty-two years of age his father pressed upon him to take holy orders, but he declined.

Now a new and powerful influence is brought to bear upon him. He reads Jeremy Taylor's *Holy Living and Dying*, then À Kempis *On the Imitation of Christ*. By these he is led to more serious thought, and to more careful vigilance over his ways. Meeting with a religious friend, his struggling convictions are strengthened, and he begins to enter in earnest upon a religious life. This is a turning-point in his religious career. It is the moment of his decision. He seeks to be a Christian not in name only. He spends an hour or two each day in retirement, he communicates every week, he watches against sin in word and work, and he begins "to aim at and pray for inward holiness."

That he reached a condition of self-satisfaction does not detract from the importance of this period of his life, nor from the reality of the work which was being silently wrought in him. He lived up to his light—it was all he could do. Clearer light will burst upon him and he will be humbled. At present he is a sincere Christian disciple, feeble it may be, and struggling; but a disciple. He is learning at the feet of a great Master.

In 1725 he took deacon's orders and preached his first sermon. In the following year he was elected to a fellowship in Lincoln; and removing to his new College, shook himself free from trifling acquaintance, and put himself under an even more rigid self-discipline. Then came another influence from another direction. His attention was arrested by Law's *Christian Perfection* and *Serious Call*, books well calculated to impress his sensitive mind in the moments of its awakening.

He becomes more and more careful in the ordering of his life. He says: "The light flowed in so mightily upon my soul that everything appeared in a new view. I cried to God for help, and resolved not to prolong the time of obeying Him as I had never done before." The struggles after a pious life were a part of the training through which he was being conducted in preparation for his great work. He could well be a teacher in religion who had been so resolute a scholar.

In 1727 he took his Master's degree, and became his father's curate for two years.

He then returned to Oxford and acted as a tutor, remaining six years.

A few words from one whom he had walked far to see must not be passed over. "Sir, you wish to serve God and go to heaven; remember you cannot serve Him alone; you must therefore *find* companions or *make* them." Dr. Abel

Stevens says, "Wesley never forgot these words, which, perhaps, forecast the history of his life."[1]

It is observable, not now only, but for some time after, how Wesley's thoughts centre on his personal salvation. His character at this time is marked by austerity and self-denial, by carefully ordered rule and method, by charity in sentiment and activities, by diligent observance of religious ordinances and all duties, and by a scrupulous buying up of time—rising early, and reading whilst either walking or riding. He is an earnest, tutored son of the Church, struggling to maintain a life of virtue and devotion. But he is far from attaining any full satisfaction, or from gaining any true repose of mind. Up to this point his aim must be interpreted by the aid of his own words.

When urged by his father to try to secure the Epworth living, he replied: "The question is not whether I could do more good to others there or here, but whether I could do more good to myself; seeing wherever I can be most holy myself, there I can most promote holiness in others."

In the year 1735 he formed the acquaintance of George Whitefield. His father died in the same year, and the home at Epworth was broken up, and he came to London.

His sympathies are now about to be drawn out towards others. He consents to be appointed as a missionary to Georgia. But even then he says: "My chief motive, to which all the rest are subordinate, is the hope of saving my own soul. I hope to learn the true sense of the gospel of Christ by preaching it to the heathen." But it must not be supposed that this prominent, if not primary purpose was the only one. He had "the hope of doing more good in

[1] *History of Methodism.*

America," and he went with this motto to guide him—*Non sibi, sed aliis* (not for one's self, but for others). But that mission was destined to do more for this future apostle than either he or any one else could have foreseen. It would lead to further steps of progress in the work of saving his own soul, and it would teach him many lessons concerning the salvation of others.

His view of the outside world was widely extended; his pity excited towards the unenlightened and untaught, and he gained a wider experience of the deceitfulness and evil which could work in the hearts even of professed Christians. No intense zeal for missionary work was kindled within him. He worked hard and faithfully, observing with the utmost strictness every detail of his duty as a clergyman. Neither obloquy nor pain, neither loss nor fatigue could hinder him from carrying out to the extreme the demands made upon him by his vows to be faithful to the laws of his Church. But for his friend Whitefield's testimony, it might be thought that little was done by him; and perhaps, as a mission, his must be held to have been a failure. His standpoint in respect of evangelical truth may be judged with some degree of accuracy from the character of a small hymn-book published by him when in Charlestown.[1]

He returned after a brief interval a wiser but not a

[1] This little hymn-book is not without its own special interest. It was the first of the long series of hymn-books bearing the name of Wesley. It has even been supposed that this was the first collection of psalms and hymns published in our language. It "strikingly illustrates his care to provide for the spiritual wants of those committed to his care, his earnest and serious temper, and his prominent ecclesiasticism." It exhibits "a strict regard to those usages of a remote antiquity to which he then attached a very exaggerated importance." (See Preface by Dr. Osborn to Reprint published by T. Woolmer.)

satisfied man. He was still very much engrossed in the great inquiry, how he could save his own soul. But a further step had been taken in the process of his preparation for his great work, at present unseen and unimagined by him. Going to Georgia had brought him into close contact with the Moravians. On the outward voyage he was struck by their calm faith in the midst of a storm, when all around were filled with fear. He carefully observed their manners, and was penetrated with admiration for them; and that he might converse with them, he learnt their language. On his return, these links drew him to Peter Böhler. Peter Böhler led John Wesley to a true faith in Jesus.

Wesley thus describes his own religious state: "I was again active in outward works, when it pleased God of His great mercy to give me twenty-six of the Moravian brethren for companions, who endeavoured to show me a more excellent way. But I understood it not at first—I was too learned and too wise, so that it seemed foolishness unto me, and I continued preaching and following after and trusting in that righteousness whereby no flesh can be justified. All the time I was at Savannah I was thus beating the air. Being ignorant of the righteousness of Christ, which, by a living faith in Him, bringeth salvation 'to every one that believeth,' I sought to establish my own righteousness, and so laboured in the fire all my days." He describes his state as one of abject bondage to sin, in which he was continually fighting, but not conquering. He says: "Before, I had willingly served sin—now, it was unwillingly; but still I served it. I fell and rose, and fell again. Sometimes I was overcome, and was in heaviness;

sometimes I overcame, and was in joy. For as in the former state I had some foretastes of the terrors of the law, so had I in this of the comforts of the gospel."—(*Journal.*)

It is not needful to tell anew the oft-told story of Wesley's conversion. We must still adhere to calling this event a "conversion." If it be said that Wesley was a Christian before, it need not be denied. But he was a very different Christian after the change had taken place from what he was before. Up to this time, with all his searching, he had not found satisfaction; he was not at rest; he had no pervading peace, no complete repose of spirit. But now all was changed. His faith was different; his views of the nature of the gospel salvation, and of the means by which it is attained, were different; himself was different; life, duty—all appeared to have passed under a transformation as great and as distinct as that which sweeps over the face of the field in the spring-time.[1] It was a new creation; he was a new "creature." To be "born again" could never afterwards be interpreted by him as a change wrought by ordinances—a baptismal change. It was no mere change of opinion, or profession, or relation to an external community. It was a spiritual change wrought by the power of God, wrought in response to a divinely-inspired faith. Judicially it was a change of relation—justified; experimentally, a change of heart—regenerated. By him the change was judged to be the greatest and most impressive that had ever occurred in his life. He had long hated and denounced sin; he had long urged home the necessity for righteousness of heart and life, both upon himself and upon all around him; but he had not until

[1] See *Works*, vol. i. p. 161.

now found the secret spring of power by which this entire change of life could be effected, the secret spring of spiritual affection, that power which, while changing the whole character of the life, should call into play the whole strength of life's energy. It was the consciousness, the happy consciousness, of reconciliation with God, the assurance of his personal salvation in Christ. "I felt that I did trust in Christ—Christ alone—for salvation; and an assurance was given me that He had taken away my sins, even *mine*, and saved *me* from the law of sin and death."

How different from his former state, concerning which he wrote (Jan. 3, 1740): "I spent two days in looking over the letters which I had received for the sixteen or eighteen years last past. How few traces of inward religion are here! I found but one among all my correspondents who declared (what I well remember at that time I knew not how to understand) that God had 'shed abroad His love in his heart,' and given him the 'peace that passeth all understanding.' But who believed his report?"—(*Works*, vol. i. p. 259.) "It is scarcely an exaggeration to say that the scene which took place at that humble meeting in Aldersgate Street forms an epoch in English history. The conviction which then flashed upon one of the most powerful and most active intellects in England is the true source of English Methodism." [1]

In analysing the essential characteristics of Methodism, it is impossible to over-estimate the importance of this event in the life of its founder—an event, let it be observed, which is found to be defined with equal clearness in the life of every one of the great Methodist leaders.

[1] *England in the Eighteenth Century*, Lecky, vol. ii. p. 558.

Charles Wesley, Whitefield, Fletcher, and their fellow-workers all passed through the same strait gate, all experienced a change which embraced the same consciousness of sin, the same self-condemnation, the same struggle after righteousness, the same faith in the atonement, the same emancipation from bondage into clear, bright, happy freedom—"no longer a servant, but a son;"—the same exuberant joy, followed by a life-long devotion to the service of God, a life-long devotion to the best interests of men. We must keep before our minds the vision of this interesting phenomenon in the religious life of the last century—the spiritual change of this man, graciously repeated in the case of every member of the entire Methodist band. But how totally unprepared was the Church of England then to receive this doctrine! How loud and violent and long-continued was the opposition raised against it, and how steadily did Wesley defend it![1]

The bearing of Wesley's conversion on the future of

[1] In drawing up a short state of the case between the clergy and himself and companions, he wrote: "About seven years since we began preaching inward, present salvation, as attainable by faith alone. For preaching this doctrine we were forbidden to preach in the churches. We then preached in private houses as occasion offered, and, when the houses could not contain the people, in the open air. For this many of the clergy preached, or printed, against us, as both heretics and schismatics. Persons who were convinced of sin begged us to advise them more particularly how to flee from the wrath to come. . . . For this we were represented, both from the pulpit and the press (we have heard it with our ears, and seen it with our eyes) as introducing Popery, raising sedition, practising both against Church and State; and all manner of evil was publicly said both of us and those who were accustomed to meet with us. . . But now several of the bishops began to speak against us, either in conversation or in public. On this encouragement several of the clergy stirred up the people to treat us as outlaws or mad dogs. The people did so both in Staffordshire, Cornwall, and many other places; and they do so still, wherever they are not restrained by their fear of the secular magistrate," etc.—(*Works*, vol. i. p. 486.)

Methodism, and, through it, on a much wider area, is very influential. To Wesley himself it represents the change which every one may, nay, must, undergo. On the forefront of his teaching in the future is inscribed the authoritative declaration, "Ye must be born again. Except a man be born of water and of the Spirit, he cannot enter into the kingdom of God." His own ineffectual struggles after righteousness are typical of the struggles of others. His own enlightenment, his own sense of repose, his quiet trust, his joy, his confidence, his clear persuasion are illustrative of conditions possible to all. And in his own errors he sees the errors of others, and is taught how to correct them. The position which a consciousness of salvation has in the Christian experience was now clearly discerned and defined. It was the comfortable assurance of present salvation in Christ, and it was an assurance which all might have. He did not regard himself as enjoying any favoured position: what was permitted to him was permitted to all. He who could sing "the hymn" for himself could cry aloud,—

"Come, all the world; come, sinner thou!
All things in Christ are ready now."

The struggles of those past days and years, and the joy of that hour of conscious salvation, were the struggles and the joy of many a soul in subsequent years. The great declaration that comes up to us from the study of this part of Wesley's life is that there is in religion something beyond even the most careful living, the most ardent zeal, the most accurate opinions. His life is ever a prominent testimony to the truth which is the burden of Methodist teaching, namely, the necessity for a distinct assurance of forgiveness of sins, in order to the attainment of the true peace and joy of the gospel. That lesson is certainly read to us and to the world by the history of the struggles of this individual soul after righteousness. After this great change had passed upon him, he, for a fortnight at least, makes entry in his journal only of his own state. Then all is hushed in a quiet assurance and confidence of faith which is never broken. This intense concentration of Wesley's thoughts on personal salvation, and the significance he 'attached to it at this time, tinge all his future work. The felt importance of his own spiritual renewal passes over into a clear apprehension of its importance to others. The path which his own feet had trodden is always a plain path for the feet of others. The bearing of all this on the future character and history of Methodism is very close. A man may teach with power that which he has himself experienced; he can scarcely go beyond that. From that hour to this the highest value has always been placed upon the individual soul, and the utmost importance attached to its salvation. Conversion is held to be, for the individual and for society, the first, the chiefest of all questions.

This is the secret spring of all—Christian conversion—the consciousness of a happy reconciliation to God. If the class-meeting is "the germ-cell"[1] of Methodism, as it has been aptly called, this is the germ, the nucleus itself. Before dealing with the evangelistic aspect of Methodism, it is necessary thus to consider the wonderful preparation of its first agents for their work, by their being led to grasp so firmly the idea of the sinner's individual con-

[1] Dr. Rigg's *Church Organizations.*

version, the permission of every sinner, the call of every sinner, to share in this blessedness.

This is the true starting-point of Methodism. It really begins here. Its first business is to proclaim the supreme importance of this. If Wesley and his companions were raised up to declare any truth, they certainly were raised up to declare this—the necessity for a conversion from sin; and the incompleteness of that conversion until it issues in a conscious reconciliation with God, until the interest of the individual in the one atonement of Jesus is a matter of clear assurance, discerned by faith, grasped, reposed in; or, as Wesley says, "a divine ἔλεγχος (*evidence or conviction*) of the love of God the Father, through the Son of His love, to him a sinner, now accepted in the Beloved." [1]

This conversion was proved to be possible independently of particular Church ordinances, although Wesley once thought "it were a sin for a soul to be saved outside a church." The unbaptized and unwashed experienced it. Hundreds were converted from gross sin to righteousness, in houses, in the fields, by the wayside. In how many instances had the ordinances of religion been vain—a mere ritual, an ineffective ritual! In how many other instances were the neglecters of public worship arrested and changed in life and character, to whom the ordinances then became a delight! It was thus declared that there was a something beyond ritual and the formalities of worship. Was all this a deceit? Let the testimony of the century declare. The abundant fruits of righteousness were there. The tree being judged by its fruits, according to a principle

[1] Sermon on "Scriptural Christianity."

enunciated by an authoritative Teacher, was it a corrupt tree that brought forth these fruits?[1]

This was the response of early Methodism to the assumptions of ritualistic and priestly exclusiveness. It could not be gainsaid. It has never been rebutted. To-day, as then, it is an unanswerable reply to all who affirm there is salvation only in *the* Church,—salvation only by ordinances administered by the hands of men who can trace their historical descent through long ages, and through the medium of men whom charity, in some instances, could hardly admit to be in the Church at all! The history of the Christian religion shows that spiritual benefits of the highest kind may be enjoyed in the complete absence of these conditions.

No Church need desire a higher authentication than the evidence that sinners are turned from the error of their ways, that they who hunger and thirst after righteousness

[1] "What Wesley and Whitefield did was due to their faithful warnings of the wrath to come, and their earnest pleadings with men that they would believe on the Lord Jesus Christ and be saved. Apart from these, their oratory would have been as sounding brass or tinkling cymbal. The rough, weather-worn cheeks of sailors and miners would not have been furrowed with tears, the hard selfishness of men of the world would not have yielded even for the moment to better impulses, the slaves of passion and vice would not have been freed from the demons which possessed them, and brought to sit at the feet of Jesus in their right minds, whole communities would not have been gathered out of the power of evil, and united by bands of faith and love for works of piety and benevolence, had these preachers addressed them as English Christians who had not been faithful to their baptismal vows, and needed to be restored to their Church by some sacrament of confession and penance. It was the emphatic and spirit-stirring proclamation of Christ as the Saviour who could deliver them from the sin in which they were plunged, and the death by which they were threatened, which made Methodism ; and if it should ever forget that truth and neglect that work, the day of its extinction will be nigh."—(*The Church Systems of England in the Nineteenth Century*, by J. Guinness Rogers, B.A., p. 584.)

are filled. This is the silent testimony of Methodism to the groundlessness of the exclusive assumptions of any Church or any congeries of Churches.

But this is also the testimony of Methodism against all latitudinarianism. To this source is to be traced the moral and social change wrought by it in the past. This is the secret spring of all its activities, of all its widespread work in the world.

This practical demonstration that the work was of God, this raising up children unto Abraham from the very stones, is afforded by Methodism from the beginning. We may point to Churches in this country, and to vast missions in other lands, which exhibit the peaceable fruits of righteousness, to multitudes taken from the lowest conditions of society and washed and made clean by its instrumentality. And all this is the fruit of a conversion which is effected by the Divine Spirit, through the preaching of "repentance toward God, and faith toward our Lord Jesus Christ."

To make definite this teaching; to demonstrate by living examples; to raise up a holy seed which by God's grace should perpetuate itself in the earth, is an essential part of the mission of Methodism. How great a mission is this! I dwell upon it, because in my judgment it is the central germ of all Methodism. It is its inner core; the secret spring of its activity, its vital essence, its very life. It is its first essential characteristic. The essence of Methodism is not in its services, even its most cherished ones, its class-meetings, its band-meetings, or its love-feasts; nor is it in the strength or peculiarities of its organization. It would be a body without a spirit in the absence of "conversion." Its ministry must be a converted ministry; a happy ministry—happy in the love of God. They must have peace with God. They must know the " witness of the Spirit," or there will be no enthusiasm for souls, no large charity, no effectual sacrifice, no crying—

> "The love of Christ doth me constrain
> To seek the wandering souls of men."

With individual adaptation to particular branches of ministerial work, it must be pre-eminently a converting ministry.

It has often been the subject of observation that Methodism provides so plentiful a supply of willing workers for the various fields of Christian service. There is but one explanation that I can give. It is all the fruit of conversion, the fruit of a conscious deliverance from sin, of a happy relation towards God, the assurance of forgiveness. This joyful consciousness of salvation lies at the foundation of all Methodist devotion. "He loved me, and gave Himself for me. I, even I, am reconciled to God by the death of His Son." It is equally so with the Christian charity which has been so largely evoked. What is the spring of the wonderful development of liberality in the manifold and great gifts of its people? It has been from the beginning almost a proverb amongst the Churches for a free and ready flow of wealth. It is no secret of Methodism. It is the true spirit of Christianity. Its spring was the same as in all other departments of service. It was the inevitable result of fervent love to the Saviour. The essence of Christianity is the essence of Methodism. It is but "Christianity in earnest"—"that form of Christianity called Methodism." Whatever is good and great in it is the common heritage of all Christians. If some fresh means of help were seized upon, they had been long lying as hid treasures in a field. It had but fulfilled its calling in returning to original principles, and bringing forth these treasures to light. This is a first distinguishing feature of Methodist teaching and experience—a happy salvation, known, exulted in, shouted over.[1]

This was no new truth, but an old one. It is taught in the best of the Church of England writings; it is embodied in the Liturgy and the Homilies. (I shall have occasion to show that Wesley always defended his position by an appeal to the authoritative writings of the Church.) It is the great cardinal doctrine of justification by faith, the doctrine of the Puritans,[2] the doctrine, the very keystone of the Reformation. It was the Pauline doctrine. But it was given to the Reformers of the eighteenth century to illustrate this great truth of salvation by faith in a clearer way than before had been done by the Churches since the Epistle to the Romans was written; and to bring it more prominently forward as the very essence of the gospel message, and the essence of that message to every soul.

[1] "Methodism grew out of the feeling that religious experience, and the truth which produces it, take precedence of everything else, and that to these primary objects all which is merely ecclesiastical must be kept in strict and lasting subordination."—(*History of Religion in England*, by Dr. Stoughton, vol. vi. p. 389.)

[2] "Wesley hated Calvinism, but the Puritan theory of the new birth was the life and soul of all his teaching."—(Rogers, p. 583.)

"As regards the spiritual nature of religion, and the necessity of conversion, they are, and always have been, Puritans of the Puritans. They have their independent opinions on Church polity, but in evangelical doctrine and practice they are Puritan, and feel that in Puritanism is their strength."—(P. 586.)

"He opposed the doctrines of predestination and perseverance, as taught by Puritans of the Commonwealth; but, notwithstanding, like John Goodwin, he had much spiritual feeling of the Puritan cast, which broke out in spite of all his antagonism to many points in Puritan theology."—(Stoughton, vol. vi. p. 120.)

How different is the conception which all the Churches now have of this doctrine from that held when the voice of this great evangelist was first heard in the land! To Methodism belongs the honour of redeeming from forgetfulness the doctrine of the necessity for spiritual conversion. This was one of the great services rendered by it to the Universal Church; and that other Churches are now teaching it with equal clearness, and contending for it with equal fervour, does not detract from its being the duty of Methodism still to give prominence to it. The clear ring of this truth was not heard in the Church. There the teaching was cold and dry. It was, as a rule, a feeble setting forth of moral duties without touching the real springs of moral power. There were a few happy exceptions, but the teachers of the day had not a true conception of the way of salvation by faith. The great effects which followed the preaching of this truth made Methodism to appear as a field which the Lord hath blessed. In it the true seeds of the kingdom had been sown; and how many of those seeds have floated in the silent evening air, and have been wafted into other fields, where they have taken root downward, and have borne fruit upward! The remarkable history of Wesley's spiritual struggle, which in so many respects was repeated in the struggles of his companions, shows in how singular a way he was fitted to be the expositor of the great doctrine. This was his early, his first message.[1]

It is here to be observed how distinctly Wesley proclaimed the doctrine of "the witness of the Spirit," using that phrase in preference to the term "assurance." He

[1] See Sermon on "Salvation by Faith," and *Works*, vol. i. p. 275.

wrote and preached upon it, and made it the subject of instruction to the Societies.

He says: "I observed many years ago, 'It is hard to find words in the language of men to explain the deep things of God. Indeed, there are none that will adequately express what the Spirit of God works in His children. But, perhaps, one might say (desiring any who are taught of God to correct, soften, or strengthen the expression), by the testimony of the Spirit, I mean an inward impression on the soul, whereby the Spirit of God immediately and directly witnesses to my spirit that I am a child of God; that Jesus Christ hath loved me and given Himself for me; that all my sins are blotted out, and I, even I, am reconciled to God.' After twenty years' further consideration, I see no cause to retract any part of this."[1]

Again he writes: "If we dwell in Christ, and Christ in us, which He will not do unless we are regenerate, surely we must be sensible of it." "That we can never be so certain of the pardon of our sins as to be assured they will never rise up against us, I firmly believe. We know that they will infallibly do so, if we apostatize; and I am not satisfied what evidence there can be of our final perseverance till we have finished our course. But I am persuaded we may know if we are *now* in a state of salvation, since that it is expressly promised in the Holy Scriptures to our sincere endeavours, and we are surely able to judge of our own sincerity."[2]

It is not surprising that the lives of the members of the Society, made so joyous, should close in equal joyousness.

---

[1] Sermon, "The Witness of the Spirit."
[2] Moore's *Life of Wesley*, vol. ii. pp. 1, 2.

One of the striking results of the Methodist teaching was found in the happy deathbeds of the people. That teaching threw a fresh glow of joy over the whole Christian experience. The Methodists were, for the most part, a happy people, notwithstanding religious struggle and difficulty. They knew the "perfect freedom" of the "service" of God. The character of their religious life may be judged by the character of the hymns which they sang, and which formed so prominent a part of their services. If Charles Wesley wrote "Hymns for Believers Mourning," he wrote more for "Believers Rejoicing." He prepared songs of triumphant exultation over death, and of bright anticipation of the felicities of the future life; his beauteous "Funeral Hymns" lighting up the gloom of the shadow of death and the very darkness of the grave, and a new song was heard on earth when he taught the people to "rejoice for a brother deceased."[1]

2. *Elevation of the Idea of Christian Life.*

I have dwelt at some length on the subject of conversion because of the importance which, in my judgment, attaches to it in the whole history of Methodism. But this is only the initial stage of the Christian life. It is right here to give prominence to a teaching which in some sense originated with Wesley; I refer to what is known as the doctrine of Christian perfection, on which

---

[1] Of these happy exultations over death—"the happy deathbeds" which characterized the early (and, thank God, do characterize the later) Methodists—Mrs. Susannah Wesley's is a beautiful example: "Children," said she, "as soon as I am released, sing a psalm," and they sung a psalm; and Charles Wesley wrote some of his most jubilant strains to sing at such times.

Wesley laid so much stress. I know exception has been taken to the use of the word perfection, and the entire doctrine has been not a little derided. Wesley's own exposition of the doctrine is the best that need be given, and his defence of it is the clearest and most conclusive.

Wesley's teaching on the loftier walks of the Christian life is the necessary complement of the doctrine of justification by faith, and follows it in natural order.

It is one of the great services rendered by Methodism to the Universal Church that, by its instrumentality, a loftier conception of the possibilities of the individual Christian life has been given to the world. It was not a loftier ideal than that which was given by the great apostle of righteousness, nor higher than that given by the apostle's Master, or by the Master's forerunner. For the utmost reach of the spiritual life and the utmost reach of Christian perfection, as taught by Wesley and his followers, finds its definition in the old words, "Thou shalt love the Lord thy God with all thy heart, and with all thy mind, and with all thy soul, and with all thy strength; and thy neighbour as thyself." Methodism never pretended to know any commandment greater than these.[1]

There is a view of this subject which I think it right to take; and it is easy to take it without abating in the least his distinctive teaching. If John Wesley was any-

---

[1] Wesley says: "By perfection I mean the humble, gentle, patient love of God and our neighbour, ruling our tempers, words, and actions. I do not include an impossibility of falling from it, either in part or in whole. Therefore I retract several expressions in our hymns which partly express, partly imply such an impossibility; and I do not contend for the term *sinless*, though I do not object against it."

thing, he was a *moral* reformer. All the doctrine that he specially developed related to the right adjustment of the Christian life. His teaching was singularly free from speculation and the fancies of imagination. It all had a practical aim and a practical tendency.[1]

[1] In "A Plain Account of Christian Perfection," in which his views are very fully given, Wesley relates with great simplicity the steps by which he was "led, during a course of many years, to embrace the doctrine," and to determine by the help of divine grace "to be all devoted to God, to give Him all my soul, my body, and my substance." He then began "not only to read, but to study the Bible, as the one, the only standard of truth, and the only model of pure religion."

"Hence," he says, "I saw, in a clearer and clearer light, the indispensable necessity of having 'the mind which was in Christ,' and of 'walking as Christ also walked,' even of having, not some part only, but all the mind which was in Him, and of walking as He walked, not only in many or in most respects, but in all things. And this was the light wherein at this time I generally considered religion, as an uniform following of Christ, an entire inward and outward conformity to our Master."

On this subject he preached before the University, on "The Circumcision of the Heart," in which he remarks, "'Love is the fulfilling of the law, the end of the commandment.' It is not only 'the first and great' command, but all the commandments in one. 'Whatsoever things are just, whatsoever things are pure, if there be any virtue, if there be any praise,' they are all comprised in this one word, love. In this is perfection, and glory, and happiness. The royal law of heaven and earth is this, 'Thou shalt love the Lord thy God with all thy heart, and with all thy soul, and with all thy mind, and with all thy strength.'"

In the following year, whilst in Savannah, he wrote:—

"Is there a thing beneath the sun,
  That strives with Thee my heart to share?
Ah! tear it thence, and reign alone,
  The Lord of every motion there!"

When returning thence, he says, "The cry of my heart was—

'O grant that nothing in my soul
  May dwell, but Thy pure love alone!
O may Thy love possess me whole,
  My joy, my treasure, and my crown!
Strange fires far from my heart remove;
  My every act, word, thought, be love!'"

He afterwards obtained from Arvid Gradin, a Moravian, the following

He early gained a conception of holiness as a practical exhibition of the Christian life. Even when he was most under the influence of the teaching of the mystics, he saw that holiness of heart could not exist without holiness of living. He never cherished a doctrinal sentiment that did not find its expression in the conduct of life. It was so with this doctrine. He held it forth as a vehement definition of "the full assurance of faith:" "Repose in the blood of Christ, a firm confidence in God, and persuasion of His favour; the highest tranquillity, serenity, and peace of mind, with a deliverance from every fleshly desire, and a cessation of all, even inward sins."

This, he says, was "the first account I ever heard from any living man of what I had before learned myself from the oracles of God, and had been praying for (with the little company of my friends) and expecting for several years."

In 1739 the brothers declared their sentiments in the words—

"Turn the full stream of nature's tide;
Let all our actions tend
To Thee, their source; Thy love the guide,
Thy glory be the end."

And—

"Lord, arm me with Thy Spirit's might,
Since I am call'd by Thy great name:
In Thee let all my thoughts unite,
Of all my works be Thou the aim:
Thy love attend me all my days,
And my sole business be Thy praise."

The first tract he wrote expressly on this subject was published in the latter end of this year. In it he largely declared his sentiments of Christian perfection. He says, "This is the very point at which I aimed all along from the year 1725, and more determinedly from the year 1730, when I began to be *homo unius libri*, 'a man of one book,' regarding none, comparatively, but the Bible. This is the very same doctrine which I believe and teach at this day."

He closes the pamphlet with the words:—"We do expect to love God with all our heart, and our neighbour as ourselves. Yea, we do believe that He will in this world so 'cleanse the thoughts of our hearts by the inspiration of His Holy Spirit, that we shall perfectly love Him, and worthily magnify His holy name.'"

protest against all Antinomian laxity and self-indulgence, affirming that it was the privilege of the Christian believer to live above sin.

That this loftier ideal of the possibilities of the Christian life was not before the eyes of the Churches at the time, is evident from the opposition so long and so loudly raised against it. It is true that the old law of love had been accepted, but neither had the area of that love been defined, nor its depths far explored. Was it believed to be an attainable condition? Had it been pressed home as a common, universal Christian privilege or a common, universal Christian duty?

It was either an undefined and indefinable height towards which all might aspire without reaching, or an equally indefinite but low estate to which any could attain without effort. Wesley, in the spirit of the most saintly Christian writers in the several periods of the Church's history, and in the several schools of religious thought, at once placed the standard high, and affirmed its attainment possible to all, and the pursuit of it obligatory upon all. It must be held to be a great and invaluable service to the race to raise the standard of its possible moral attainment. To abate that standard in any degree would inflict an incalculable injury on human society. Every man who goes beyond his fellows in the exhibition of some high quality of personal character lays the whole world under tribute to him. Every skilful performance, every act of self-sacrificing charity, every deed of heroism or of self-denying service, every example of unsullied purity or of large charity, exalts the standard up towards which a slow world creeps.

If Wesley had not illustrated in his life what he taught by his pen, he would have given to the world but a meagre representation of the great truth. But he not only taught the doctrine—he exhibited it; yet without any boastful assertion of its attainment. And he was delicately sensitive to the danger of preaching a holiness that had not both its description and its warrant in Scripture. It was his aim, as he felt it to be his calling, "to spread *scriptural* holiness over the land." Then, by reverent preaching and faithful practice, he commended the doctrine to all.

If some could not hear the sounds of the well-tuned harp making melody before God in the secrecies of his heart's sanctuary, they could see the well-trained hand in its ceaseless, unwearied service to his fellow-man; and all done in love and for love. It was not difficult to catch the teaching of, "I have four silver spoons, two here and two at Bristol, and by the grace of God I will have no more so long as so many lack bread." There is no more distinct and convincing proof of a man's whole-hearted love of God than this serviceable love of man for God's sake.

The insistence on this truth must be regarded as an essential characteristic of Methodism; but it would be a faulty view of it did we not take into consideration the call to Christian activity as a part of the real Christian perfection, and a proof of it.

Wesley has been ridiculed for his teaching on "Christian perfection," almost if not quite as much as for his belief in the Epworth Ghost. Be it so. If his nomenclature has in some instances appeared to be in fault, as some have affirmed, though it would be difficult to rebut his own defence of it; and if the examples of Christian perfection, or "perfect love,"[1] have been thought to be so few and the faults of some of its professors all too apparent, yet the Churches have paid their silent tribute to the truth by holding up to view, and holding out for acceptance, the gracious permission. In our day some of the sweetest songs of the sanctuary are the expression of whole-hearted consecration to the service of God, and full-hearted experience of the soul's rapt satisfaction with the love of God, and full-handed service in the Lord's name to the needy, or suffering, or sinful fellow-man; whilst on every hand illustrative examples occur in all the Churches of a practical ministry of love bearing witness to the reality and perfectness of a professed, a happy, a mystical enjoyment of love. Many a son of Asaph has sung Charles Wesley's hymns on "Full Redemption," or written others which, if they have equalled them in bold assertion of the richness of the Christian calling, have fallen behind them only in clearness of exposition, in depth of discernment, and in felicity of spiritual expression.

Methodism has not been altogether unfaithful to this trust; and even where the confession of the doctrine has not been followed up by the faithful pursuit of the experience in the life, the neglected privilege has lain, like an unearned prize, a condemnation of the indolence which failed to gain it. Let it be a reproach to us that this is a distinctive doctrine of Methodism—rather let me say a glory of our theology, and a reproach to us that, whilst with our lips we have confessed such a state attainable, with our lives we have so often contradicted

[1] "In him verily hath the love of God been perfected" (1 John ii. 5)

the confession. But the glory has not departed from us. Never since Wesley's days was the doctrine more faithfully, if sometimes unwisely, taught or more urgently pressed home upon the acceptance of believers; while in many an unostentatious life it is beautifully and simply illustrated.

3. *Evangelism.*

After the conversion of the Wesleys and of Whitefield, Methodism burst into life. Everything previously was in an embryo state, finding its analogy in those great changes which are observable in external nature when, as in the growth of the grain, slow and silent preparatory processes are carried forward unseen until the favourable moment arrives for their revelation. Beneath the surface of the soil, the hidden germ swells and grows, its processes multiplying as its unfolding life advances, until at length the growing blade, urged forward by the forceful vital principle, pierces the brown earth, and, bursting through every impediment, leaves the darkness of the ground for the clear bright light and the pure air of heaven.

We find Wesley immediately after the great change retiring for three months into Germany, and, in his retirement, holding quiet converse with the Moravians, from whom he had already derived so great benefit. Their spirit, their manners and habits, and the features of their church-life arrest his attention. He is open and sensitive to any good influence. He receives the impress of this simple people; and in his heart are sown the seeds of the future

Christian community it would be his calling and honour to form.¹

Wesley returned to England on Saturday, September 16th, 1738. On the following day he began, as he says, to declare in his "own country the glad tidings of salvation, preaching three times, and afterwards expounding the holy gospel to a large company in the Minories." Thus at once, with an energy which never slackened, began the labour of more than fifty years spent in the endeavour to evangelize his native land.

On the last day of the year he preached "to many thousands in St. George's, Spitalfields, and to a yet more crowded congregation at Whitechapel in the afternoon." At midnight a little company of evangelists, clergy of the Church of England, and nearly sixty members of a small Society, met in Fetter Lane. The service was very remarkable. It continued until three o'clock in the morning. Hearken! "As we were continuing instant in prayer, the power of God came mightily upon us, insomuch that

¹ There are interesting links of relation between Methodism and another great work of another Oxford student. Wesley's work is by lineal descent to be traced from that of England's earlier reformer, Wycliffe, whose doctrines Jerome of Prague carried from Oxford to Bohemia, whence followed a great Reformation, with John Huss (to whom Wycliffe's doctrines were so dear) at its head. After the faithful martyr's death some of his followers moved from Moravia to Herrnhut, in Lusatia, and founded there the Moravian settlement, the very mention of which brings many names (Peter Böhler conspicuously) and many incidents to our thoughts—*e.g.* the exposition of Luther's Preface to the little Society in Aldersgate Street. So, although Wesley was the debtor to the Moravians, they were debtors to Wycliffe. Alike in their recognition of the supreme authority of Holy Scripture, in their power as preachers of righteousness, and in their employment of itinerant evangelists both lay and cleric ; and alike as instruments honoured of God for reviving His work in the earth, Wycliffe laboured to purify the doctrine, Wesley the manners—the life of the Church.

many cried out for exceeding joy, and many fell to the ground. As soon as we were recovered a little from that awe and amazement at the presence of His Majesty, we broke out with one voice, 'We praise Thee, O God; we acknowledge Thee to be the Lord.'"

So began that year from which is to be dated the great religious awakening which, to use the language of Isaac Taylor, "has immediately or remotely so given an impulse to Christian feeling and profession on all sides that it has come to present itself as the starting-point of our modern religious history."

On the 5th of the same month seven clergymen met at Islington. They continued in fasting and prayer until three o'clock in the morning, and broke up "with a full conviction that 'God was about to do great things.'"[1] Whitefield was there, and John and Charles Wesley, and others whose names are not so familiar.

Now the imprisoned spirit bursts forth. These men feel that they have a gospel to preach, a gospel of God, such a gospel as their fellow-countrymen need; and that they have a commission and a command to preach it. We see the little band of devoted clergymen, happy in the first experiences of their new life, giving themselves to fervent evangelistic work. It is the natural outcome of the great change they have all felt. "They had themselves deep experience of the power and joy of that salvation which they preached to others."[2] One supreme force drives them along—the love of God; the love of man. This is their first impulse, the impulse of a vital Christianity. Their final aim is the universal diffusion of

[1] Whitefield's *Journal*.   [2] Rogers, p. 138.

the blessings of that Christianity. What they do, they do as a duty, and they are accustomed to obey the behests of duty; they had had an effective training in this, and they do it with joy. They do it also as a charity. With a pitiful and tender compassion for the outcasts they cry

> "The love of Christ doth me constrain
> To seek the wandering souls of men."

They saw their fellow-countrymen in wretchedness extreme. They had a remedy in their hands. They had a truth, a supreme truth—the possibility of all, each, every one, attaining to a consciousness of salvation, of reconciliation with God, of freedom from the dominion of the sin which they saw was holding down and trampling under foot much of the best life of the English nation. They had a happy, joyous, effective salvation for every one. They knew that wherever they went the wilderness might blossom as the rose; and they saw what they believed to be the direct tokens of the divine approval of their labours, in the great changes wrought by their preaching.

These evangelists fall to their work with a mighty energy, preaching with great fervour in the churches, which became crowded with eager, listening multitudes. They seek the spiritual redemption of the poor and ignorant and brutal around them. This is their hope; this their labour, and, by God's blessing, this they attain. Men are rescued and changed, as they believe, by divine grace operating through their instrumentality. Hundreds of people are converted. This to them is the signature of the divine approval of their work. They want no more.

Soon, however, the doors of the churches are closed

against them. Then the grand departure is made. In February of this year Whitefield, in March John, and in June Charles Wesley are preaching in the fields. From this moment the great work enters upon a new phase.

One of the features of Wesley's great reformation was that it was done without a previously devised plan. The one purpose to which I have given prominence led to everything. It was "not by might, nor by power." A handful of men, inspired by the Spirit that moved ancient prophets, and apostles, and evangelists, went up and down the country preaching the gospel, and seeking to revive primitive Christianity in the old historic Church of the land, and to spread it abroad as, according to its original purpose, it was to be spread, urged by an impulse they dared not resist. " God thrust us out against our will to raise up a holy people." They longed for the renewal of the Church in her beauty and sanctity. They would fain have spent their strength within her borders. But no: the Church was not at the time fitted to receive them; and she closed her doors against them. "Church or no Church," was their cry, "we must save souls." And out they went. The churchyard, the highway, the field, the market-place, the broad road—anywhere where there was a wall to stand on or a space for the people in which to gather, was a suitable place for their labour.

Ah! the closing of the church doors opened other doors; the way was made clear to the masses of the people, who, alas! never darkened the church portals.

A new career opens to these fervent evangelists.

They are no longer bound. Without any design on their part they are compelled to retire from the churches to publish the gospel to the multitudes outside. The opposition of the clergy, in refusing the use of their pulpits to the "Methodists," turned out to the furtherance of the great work.[1] That which could not have been effectually done within the walls of the building was to be done without, in the open fields and market-places. We see Wesley, the stickler for order, who but now thought "the saving of souls almost a sin if it had not been done in a church," standing on a hillock and proclaiming the glad tidings of salvation to 3000 people; and Whitefield, the leader in this daring, this holy innovation, with a company of 10,000 around him; and Charles, who held back, at length standing on " George Whitefield's pulpit—the wall."

Two causes co-operated to lead to this result—the inward impulse which since the "conversion" has been as a fire within their bones, compelling them to speak; and the external interdict, forbidding them to speak within the churches.

This is the supreme moment in the history of the great revival. Mr. Rogers is correct. " It is not too much to say that, apart from open-air preaching, Methodism would never have had an existence."

Let us mark the words in which this illustrious trio describe their entering upon such heroic work. White-

---

[1] "It is not Methodism alone, but the nation, the world, the sacred cause of Christianity, that has gained by the harsh usage, which, in driving John Wesley out of the pale of Church life, snapped the fetters which else might have bound him, and sent him forth disinherited and disowned, but independent and free."—(Rogers, p. 570.)

field, the leader in this bold step, tells his story in great simplicity. "To-day my Master, by His providence and Spirit, compelled me to preach in the churchyard of Islington. To-morrow I am to repeat that mad trick, and on Sunday to go out into Moorfields."—(*Letter.*) "Sunday, April 29. Begun to be yet more vile this day."

John Wesley writes: "Monday, April 2. At four in the afternoon, I submitted to be more vile, and proclaimed in the highways the glad tidings of salvation, speaking from a little eminence in a ground adjoining to the city to about 3000 people."[1]

Charles Wesley gives this account of his struggle and decision: "My inward conflict continued. I perceived it was the fear of man, and that by preaching in the field next Sunday, as George Whitefield urges me, I shall break down the bridge and become desperate." He retired, and prayed for particular direction, offering up friends, liberty, life itself for Christ's sake and the gospel's. On the following day, Sunday, June 24, he adds, "The first scripture I cast my eye upon was, 'Then came the servant unto him, and said, Master, what shall we do?' I prayed with West, and went forth in the name of Jesus Christ. I found near 10,000 helpless sinners waiting for the word in Moorfields. I invited them in my Master's words as well as name: 'Come unto Me, all ye that travail and are heavy laden, and I will give you rest.' The Lord was with me, even me, His meanest messenger, according to His promise. At St. Paul's the psalms, lessons, etc., for the day, put

[1] *Works*, vol. i. p. 185.

fresh life into me. So did the sacrament. My load was gone, and all my doubts and scruples. God shone upon my path, and I knew this was His will concerning me."[1]

Methodism becomes instantly, without pre-arrangement, and in a far wider and more distinctive degree than its founders had yet contemplated, and by the force of overwhelming circumstances, *an Evangelism*—a great evangelistic mission. It will come to be proven that this is the greatest work of Methodism. To this it is called. It is its mission—undefined at present. Methodism itself is not defined, even in the minds of its leaders. There is indeed no Methodism as yet. It is the holy zeal of a few clergymen of the Church of England, fired by a true, a deep, a vital experience of the power of the gospel, fulfilling the vows and obligations of their ordination. These chosen instruments, pre-eminently fitted and prepared for a great work, are literally thrust out, thrust out against their will (as Wesley says) to the needy, the careless, the unsaved thousands of the land.

We now watch Wesley and his coadjutors working on with amazing zest, and with marked singleness of purpose. They preach literally in the highways. They preach the redemption by themselves but newly experienced. They preach salvation to all men. They preach it in opposition to rude sinfulness and to careless indifferentism, and to the self-satisfied moralism of the day, in opposition to Anglican sacramentarianism and to the prevalent restrictive and exclusive Calvinism. The Wesleys and Whitefield knew that they had a divine Evangel to proclaim. They knew what was meant by its being "the power of God unto

[1] *Journal*, vol. i. p. 155.

salvation" to him that believeth. This they had proved it to be in their own hearts. The gospel was the divinest fact to them. This was "the fiery torch" which, as Mr. Leslie Stephen says, "was borne throughout the land by them and by the numerous itinerant preachers who followed their example with much zeal, if with little learning." "This," to use the words of Dr. Dale, "is that gospel by which under God the evangelical revival recovered a large part of this country from heathenism, and restored the faith and rekindled the zeal of decaying Churches."[1] Here are the bubbling waters in the leafy pools, at the very head of the flowing stream of the "Old Evangelicalism."[2]

It would seem that for some time they had but one idea. They thought not of the external tendencies of their work. That which to them was first, both in order of importance and in order of time, was *the saving of souls*. This was the true evangelism. This is and ever must be the one first, chief work of Methodism, if it is to remain Methodism—to save souls as Wesley thought of the saving of souls—the convicting men of their sinfulness, the persuading them to its abandonment, the guiding them to the cross to obtain justification through faith in a crucified Redeemer, the leading them to renewal by the grace of the Holy Spirit, to consecration to the divine service, to the maintenance of good works, to growth in knowledge and grace, and to the aiming at entire sanctification or perfect love.

This is the foremost mission of Methodism. The highest

---

[1] *The Old Evangelicalism and the New*, p. 58.
[2] Appendix A, by the Rev. R. W. Dale, D.D.

type of a Methodist is he who has this zealous passion for souls.

Wesley fixed the eye of his preachers on this one object as the chief end of their labour. "You have nothing to do but to save souls," was as deeply embedded in the convictions of the founders of Methodism as it came to be clearly written in their rules. It was the only addition made to a collection of "Rules for a Helper," which Wesley at an early period drew up. To this they lent themselves; for this they spared no time, nor labour, nor strength, nor life itself.

In due time these men will bring many ameliorating and educative influences to bear upon the people, but for the present they are intent on the one work—the saving the soul. Men are perishing in the waves. The first business is to rescue them—to lift them up upon the beach and restore to them animation. To wash, to clothe, to feed, to recover the lost strength are secondary considerations: heed will be given to them in due time. They had one grand truth, first in importance. What a truth it was to bring to the wretched of that day! It is precious for any day and for any people; but more especially to men sunken in the wretchedness of degrading sin. In this they could not be restrained. The anger of mobs, the coldness of the worldly, the rude usage of the brutal, and the general supineness, all seemed but powers to arouse them and stimulate them to greater endeavours, to a more intense and fervently devoted zeal. The condition of these men seems to have its counterpart in that of the earlier servants of the same Master, the first publishers of the same gospel, when they went forth amongst the blind and maimed, the sick and dying, and were told to heal the one and give sight to the other, to cast out devils, and having freely received, freely to give.

The devotion of these consecrated lives to the lofty end, the evangelization of the people; the willing submission to the uncompromising sway of this purpose on the part of the makers of Methodism, is a sublime picture to contemplate. Wesley was, in some respects, the brightest example of this. He never wavered from it. His literary sympathies, his great literary labours, his power of organization, and the demand for it, his tendency to methodical procedure, the ever-widening extent of his toils, never diverted his heart from this central purpose, or weakened his energy in its pursuit for one moment. George Whitefield, by his impassioned, flame-like appeals to sinners to repent, poured out his life a sacred and a willing libation in the service of his race. Charles Wesley, not a whit behind in either fervour or fidelity, added the charm of his sacred song an offering upon the same altar, giving point by his mellifluous verse to his tender and loving appeals :—

"Come, sinners, to the gospel feast;
Let every soul be Jesu's guest."

When afterwards the little company met in conference, by a rigid catechetical method, the same object was always kept before them. All arrangements were made to promote this end. When they considered the establishment of the Society, with its elaborate organization of classes and bands for men and for women, for penitents and for believers, with its array of officers, the same end was always held in view. And even when it was found that this object must draw others in its train, and that it could not be effectually accomplished without a very wide range of spiritual work, this was the guiding and controlling idea. Whatever method or plan they adopted was adopted because of its practical bearing on the one work in hand. Probably there never has been since the days of the apostles a band of men so completely devoted to the fulfilling of the command, "Go ye: preach the gospel;" so unselfish in their spirit; so persistent in their obedience to this high commission, and at the same time so largely successful in carrying it out, as were these men, who thus stamped upon Methodism for all time as one of its essential characteristics—a devout and a fervent evangelism.

There is a feature of Methodism which must not escape our observation. I refer to its restless activity. It is an almost perennial restlessness. Wesley never designed his assistants to be settled in any sense. Himself an almost marvellous illustration of activity, he made rules for his helpers, which, if observed, would certainly prevent them from stagnation and indolence. He judged that the great work to be done was a work which demanded the most entire devotion of body and mind, of time and possessions, of which devotion he was himself so brilliant an example. This was of the essence of Methodism. It is embedded in its form as it is embodied in its regulations :—"Let every Methodist preacher consider himself as called to be, in point of enterprise, zeal, and diligence, a home missionary, and to enlarge and extend as well as keep the Circuit to which he is appointed." It was not the fulfilment of a prescribed routine of duty, but a whole-hearted, whole-bodied devotion to this one work, than which they had nothing else to do—" not to preach so many sermons, but to save as many souls as you can."

Of course the saving of souls from sin is presumably an object common to all the Churches; but there is a difference between such an object coming in as one of many judged to be equally important, and receiving equal attention, and the having this as the one supreme and ruling passion. The flag of Methodism still has this emblazoned upon it. Individual Methodists, whether within or without the ministry, may be unfaithful to it; the Connexion at large may for a time be forgetful of it. But it has not hitherto been forgotten—very far from it—even where the wider culture of the Church has claimed a large measure of attention; for the true spirit of Methodism can never be satisfied without it. One cannot help seeing that there runs through all the labours of Wesley and the early and even later Methodists, a call to the Churches to devote themselves to active evangelism, to consider and care for the outcasts. This is the teaching of the old field-preaching; this the teaching of the numerous Christian activities set agoing by Methodism in the past and present centuries; and it is universally admitted that the revived and active state of the Churches to-day is due in a very large degree to the contagion of that example it was the honour of Methodism to give.

4. *Fellowship—the Society.*

It soon became apparent to the keen eye of the leader of the holy crusade that the people who gathered around his standard, though converted from the error of their ways, and recovered from the follies and the filth of sinfulness, were yet untutored in spiritual truth, undisciplined by spiritual experience, and undefended by spiritual association. He saw that they needed a defence from temptation, from the discouragements which untoward surroundings or the fluctuations in their religious feelings might occasion, from the erroneous views which unhappily were freely floating in the air; and, moreover, that they in their ignorance needed a process of teaching in scriptural doctrine and in the principles of Christian life and duty. He had known the dangers of discouragement and loneliness; he had tasted the bitterness of spiritual depression; and, according to a prevailing and guiding principle, he found in the necessities of his own spiritual life a key to the wants of others.

It was further evident to him that the community of believers would be the most effectual support of individuals, who, separate and alone, were without strength, but united, might become powerful. He did not forget the words of one who assured him if he would go to heaven he must go in company. In fellowship, strength would be gained, and the feeble and lonely would be sheltered and cheered. Besides which, he had been much in communion with the Moravian Society. He had seen the manner of life of this interesting people, and the follies and vagaries of a few of their number could not blind him to the excellences of the many, or hide from him the true character of the principles of a Church, the beauty of whose fellowship and the power of whose doctrines had so deeply impressed him.

All these were guiding lines leading him towards the formation of his Society, to the idea of which, when once entertained, he adhered with great tenacity; every fresh development of method but strengthening and confirming him in his original plan. In addition to all this he had knowledge of the successful experiment which had been made in different parts of the country, especially in those Societies which were identified with the names of Dr. Woodward and Dr. Horneck.

The formation of the Society has its own intrinsic interest, and its character may perhaps best be disclosed by tracing its growth. Wesley tells us, in the utmost simplicity,[1] that the effect of his own and his brother's preaching was that the hearts of many were influenced, as well as their understandings, and they determined to follow Christ. And, he says, " One, and another, and another came to us, asking what they should do, being distressed on every side. We advised them, ' Strengthen you one another. Talk together as often as you can. And pray earnestly with and for one another, that you may endure to the end and be saved.' " But they said: "We want you likewise to talk with us often, to direct and quicken us in our way, to give us the advices which you well know we need, and to pray with us as well as for us." " I asked," he adds, " Which of you desire this ? Let me know your names and places of abode. They did so. But I soon found they were too many for me to talk with severally so often as they wanted it. So I told them, ' If you will all of you come together every Thursday in the evening, I will gladly spend some time with you in prayer, and give you the best advice I can.' Thus arose, without any previous design on either side, what was afterwards called a Society."

This account corresponds with that prefixed to the " Rules

[1] *Works*, vol. viii. p. 249.

of the Society." He "appointed a day when they might all come together; which from thenceforward they did every week, viz. on Thursday in the evening." This occurred in the latter end of the year 1739. It was the rise of what afterwards came to be called "The United Societies."

Very suggestively, Wesley adds: "Upon reflection I could not but observe, This is the very thing which was from the beginning of Christianity. In the earliest times, those whom God had sent forth 'preached the gospel to every creature.' And the οἱ ἀκροαταί, 'the body of hearers,' were mostly either Jews or heathens. But as soon as any of these were so convinced of the truth as to forsake sin and seek the gospel salvation, they immediately joined them together, took an account of their names, advised them to watch over each other, and met these κατηχούμενοι, 'catechumens' (as they were then called), apart from the great congregation, that they might instruct, rebuke, exhort, and pray with them and for them, according to their several necessities."[1]

The period lying between the latter end of 1739 and the 20th of July, 1740, was one of great trial and strife, in consequence of the prevalence of strange mystic opinions amongst the Moravians at Fetter Lane, with whom Wesley was associated. On the latter date, finding that he could not convince them of their error, and after many ineffectual attempts to bring them to a better mind, he withdrew from them, as did eighteen or nineteen of the Society.[2] On the

---

[1] "A Plain Account of the People called Methodists," *Works*, vol. viii. pp. 249-251.

[2] A very tender and touching appeal is made to them, and an account is given of his struggle in an extract from his *Journal*, from November 1, 1739, to September 3, 1741. This was a dissent and a protest against the error,

following Wednesday, July 23, 1740, the little company of seceders met for the first time in a building that afterwards became famous in the history of Methodism, an old disused "Foundery" in Moorfields, instead of at Fetter Lane.[1] This was the beginning of the *Wesleyan* Methodist Society. There had been already an Oxford, and subsequently, a Moravian Methodism.

These Moravian difficulties introduced by Molther were the first impeding obstacle to the progress of the work that sprang up within the Society. They had the effect of entirely diverting Wesley's course. But what seemed to arise from evil was overruled to good. Wesley was thrown out of alliance with a small people, who by the peculiarities of their Church organization, their restricted views, the rigidity of their methods, and their strong hold upon his sympathies, might have cramped within narrow limits a work which was destined to a world-wide extension and adaptation. The Moravians still meet in Fetter Lane: the Wesleyan Methodist Societies are in all the ends of the earth.

The Society was now established in its freedom and independence, with its great leader at its head; and he was uncontrolled. He writes: "Our little company met at the Foundery, instead of Fetter Lane. About twenty-five of our brethren God hath given us already, all of whom think and speak the same thing."[2] From this small beginning has the great work spread. "The kingdom of heaven is like unto a grain of mustard seed, which indeed is less

and a separation from a people whom Wesley on many grounds both loved and esteemed.—(*Works*, vol. i. p. 245.)

[1] *Works*, vol. i. p. 283.
[2] *Journal*, Wednesday, July 23, 1740.

than all seeds; but when it is grown, it is greater than the herbs, and becometh a tree."[1]

It appears there was one meeting of the Society each week; and Wesley visited the members at their own homes. This he continued to do even when the numbers had greatly increased. But as the people were scattered "from Wapping to Westminster," he soon found that he could not easily see what the behaviour of each person in his own neighbourhood was. The work was too great even for his activity. Then it was that "the Bristol plan" was adopted in London. That plan of dividing the Society into little companies or classes under a lay leader was initiated in Bristol, on February 15, 1742. As we all know, this plan was merely an arrangement to facilitate the collection of a sum of money needed to meet a debt incurred in the erection of the first "meeting-house," the one still standing in Broad Mead. But Wesley soon saw in this a means to a greater end; and, calling the Bristol leaders together, he desired that each would make particular inquiry into the behaviour of those he saw weekly.

In a little more than a month from this division of the Bristol Society into classes he writes in relation to the Society in London (March 25, 1742): "I appointed several earnest and sensible men to meet me, to whom I showed the great difficulty I had long found of knowing the people who desired to be under my care. After much discourse they all agreed there could be no better way to come to a sure, thorough knowledge of each person than to divide them into classes, like those at Bristol, under the inspection of those in whom I could most confide. This was the origin of

[1] Matt. xiii. 31, 32.

our classes at London, for which," he adds, "I can never sufficiently praise God, the unspeakable usefulness of the institution having ever since been more and more manifest."

Each class, numbering about twelve individuals, was under the care of a leader, whose business it was to see each member of his class once a week. At first the leaders visited each person at his own house; but this was soon found, on many grounds, not to be expedient, and therefore it was agreed that those of each class should meet together; and so the weekly meetings of the classes began. At first many were extremely averse to meeting thus. Some viewed it not as a privilege (as Wesley says, "indeed an invaluable one"), but rather a restraint, and, as they did not like to be restrained in anything, objected to the change on that account. Some were ashamed to speak before company; others complained of the unsuitability of the leaders; others, again, honestly said, "I do not know why, but I do not like it;" while some objected, "There were no such meetings when I came into the Society first, and why should there now?"[1] Some of these objections are re-echoed to-day; but now, as then, many prove the inestimable benefit of these "little meetings." Wesley again and again saw the usefulness of the class-meeting, and wrote in its defence.

We do not claim for Wesley any originality of design in grouping his converts in Societies. This had been done before his time—done, indeed, as he saw, in the very earliest hours of the Christian Church. For what is the Christian Church, after all, but a number of religious societies, more or less organized, and bound together by ties

[1] *Works*, vol. viii. pp. 253-255.

of sympathy, by common interests and common aims? But the way in which he was led ultimately to divide his converts into little companies is a singular evidence of his wisdom in perceiving the utility of suggested means and of the gracious overruling of Divine Providence, Whose wise workings found in him so ready and obedient a servant. The practical sagacity displayed by Wesley in laying hold upon whatever seemed likely to aid in the general purpose of guarding and tutoring the individual believer, and of calling out the individual gift for the common good, is universally acknowledged.[1]

Wesley laid down as the one only condition required of those who sought admission into his Society, "a desire to flee from the wrath to come, and to be saved from their sins"—a sense of danger, of need; a desire for help. He believed that he could render that help. Those who came to him first and asked him to meet them had this desire. They were awakened to a knowledge of their sinfulness, their need and peril, by the new preaching. It was their cry and desire that led him to form the Society. He did not go forth with any prearranged purpose to form one.[2] It arose from the depths of need. To meet that need he saw nothing better than, "Come to me, as many of you as thus feel, on Thursday evening, and I will advise you." It was a simple expedient to meet a simple want. Nothing

[1] Small companies of the Society *met* in "bands" in Bristol and in London before the Society was divided into classes, and therefore before the classes met as such; and there were stewards of the Society, and leaders of the bands; and tickets were given in the "bands" at Kingswood as early as February 24, 1741. (See *Journal*, Sept. 6, 1740; January 4, Feb. 28, March 30, April 7, May 23, July 31, 1741.)

[2] "Thus arose, without any previous design on either side, what was afterwards called *a Society*."

else was required of all who asked *admission* than a desire to save the soul: no other demand was made of any who knocked at that gate.

But if they desired to *continue* in the Society, three things were expected of them—1, forsaking of all evil; 2, doing all possible good; 3, attendance upon the ordinances of religion, including the sacrament of the Lord's Supper. These were the terms of continuous membership in the Society. It may be proper here to remark that no reference is made to Church membership. Wesley never said or implied that membership in his Societies was in itself Church membership. But it involved Church membership somewhere, according to what he judged to be Church membership, which required the hearing the pure word and receiving the sacraments; and we have no other definition from Wesley's pen,[1] save that beautifully spiritual definition given in his sermon "Of the Church,"—"The catholic or universal Church is, all the persons in the universe whom God hath so called out of the world as to entitle them to the preceding character," etc.[2]

Wesley does not undertake to defend the accuracy of the Church of England definition in all particulars, although he adopted it without alteration into the Service Book prepared by him for the American Churches.[3]

[1] "*Q.* What is a member of the Church of England?—*A.* A believer hearing the pure word of God preached, and partaking of the sacraments, duly administered in that Church."—(*Min. Conf.*, 1744.)

[2] *Works*, vol. vi. p. 397.

[3] "The Church of England is that body of men in England in whom 'there is one Spirit, one hope, one Lord, one faith;' which have 'one baptism,' and 'one God and Father of all.' This, and this alone, is the Church of England, according to the doctrine of the apostle. But the definition of a Church laid down in the Article includes not only this, but much more, by that remarkable addition: 'In which the pure word of God is

But unquestionably with him attendance on the Lord's Supper implied Church membership in the visible Church of Christ.[1] Such attendance was obligatory on the members of the Society, and, as I have said, implied Church membership somewhere, but not in the Society, for he did not allow his preachers to administer the sacraments. Of course, the greater number of the members of his Societies were members of the Church of England. Some were members of other Churches, but without such membership they could not continue to be members of the Society, if the rules were observed.

This was certainly the case until in London or Bristol the sacrament was administered to the Society by him or his brother or some other clergyman. But years elapsed before

preached, and the sacraments be duly administered.' According to this definition, those congregations in which the pure word of God (a strong expression) is not preached are no parts either of the Church of England or the Church Catholic, as neither are those in which the sacraments are not duly administered. I will not undertake to defend the accuracy of this definition. I dare not exclude from the Church Catholic all those congregations in which any unscriptural doctrines, which cannot be affirmed to be 'the pure word of God,' are sometimes, yea, frequently, preached; neither all those congregations in which the sacraments are not 'duly administered.' Certainly if these things are so, the Church of Rome is not so much as a part of the Catholic Church, seeing therein neither is 'the pure word of God' preached, nor the sacraments 'duly administered.' Whoever they are that have 'one Spirit, one hope, one Lord, one faith, one God and Father of all,' I can easily bear with their holding wrong opinions, yea, and superstitious modes of worship. Nor would I, on these accounts, scruple still to include them within the pale of the Catholic Church; neither would I have any objection to receive them, if they desired it, as members of the Church of England.' —(*Works*, vol. vi. p. 397.)

This extract bears witness alike to his precision in defining his views, and to his broad charity and catholicity of spirit.

[1] "But if they are visibly joined by assembling together to hear His word, and partake of His Supper, they are then a visible Church."—(" Earnest Appeal," *Works*, vol. viii. p. 31.)

this could be the case with the Societies generally. Indeed, he did not make provision until near the close of his life for the sacrament to be given to the Societies by any but by clergymen.

As we hear nothing of members of the Methodist *Church* in Wesley's day, so we hear nothing of the like afterwards for a long time.

After Wesley's death, when the Societies came to be dealt with as Churches, and the sacraments were administered to them by their own preachers, the members of the Societies became *ipso facto* Church members according to Wesley's own accepted definition of Church membership. Thus it was that the Methodist Societies became the Methodist Churches. By the very fact of administering to them the sacraments Wesley constituted them Churches; and all that the Conference did afterwards was to extend this to all the Societies. Members of other Churches, or attendants on other ministries, were still admitted into the Society if they had the desire to save their own souls; and if they remained in the Society, they must, according to the rules, take the Lord's Supper either in their own congregation or in some other. It cannot be doubted that the Society then fulfilled the conditions of Church membership; nor can it be doubted, except on certain High Church principles, that the Society was a Church, although it was not called one. But the idea of membership in the Society was prominent, not the idea of Church membership. And this continued until very recently. In fact, at the present time many retain this view.[1]

---

[1] But see *Wesleyan Methodism regarded as the System of a Christian Church*, by Rev. William H. Rule, 1846.

Essential Characteristics. 51

Another peculiarity is observable. From the early times of Methodism until comparatively recent years, the Society ticket was shown at the sacrament of the Lord's Supper; but members of other Churches desired to join in the Eucharistic feast with the Methodists, and they had not tickets to present. It was therefore determined, in 1796, that tickets should be given to all communicants not being members of the Society, and so they could show them as the members did.

This then came to be the actual state of things; the members of the Society attended the sacrament in the church, until they could have it in the chapel, because of their Society relationship (perhaps this may have led in some degree to the greater prominence given to the idea of the Society); and members of other Churches, whether members of the Society or not, joined them.

But another change seems gradually to have followed. These communicants' tickets were given to some persons who were not members of any Church, and not members of the Methodist Societies, and they were admitted to the Lord's Table, practically constituting them members of the Church, in fellowship with the Methodists. This was the condition of things when prominence began to be given to the idea of the Methodist *Church*, a phrase now becoming common in our official documents, although the Conference has never formally defined the Methodist Church.

The present problem, which some urge for speedy solution, is how to maintain the Society with its classes intact, and at the same time provide for the admission to the Lord's Table and to the privileges of Church membership of those who, being wishful to lead a godly life, and willing to submit to Church discipline, do nevertheless not feel free to meet in class.

Fellowship with the Society by means of the class-meeting (or its equivalent) stands forth as an essential characteristic of Methodism. It is its strongest bond of union; its most effective means of spiritual improvement and culture; its most successful method of bringing the Church members into close intercourse on spiritual things; and it is its most effectual way of guarding each individual believer, and of securing mutual help, consideration, and care. It affords the opportunity for true spiritual oversight, and an actual brotherly communion. While it declares the common interests of all, it takes careful cognizance of each. Every sheep in the flock is known and named and numbered; every one is watched over and accounted for: no one is too mean to be recorded.

How great was the necessity for some such provision as this! What opportunity was there before for the true fellowship of believers, or for mutual spiritual service? The Church was as a field untilled, a power unemployed. "Which of those true Christians had any such fellowship with these? Who watched over them in love? Who marked their growth in grace? Who advised and exhorted them from time to time? Who prayed with them and for them, as they had need? This, and this alone, is Christian fellowship. But, alas! where is it to be found? Look east or west, north or south—name what parish you please: is this Christian fellowship there? Rather, are not the bulk of the parishioners a mere rope of sand? What Christian connexion is there between them? What intercourse in spiritual things? What watching over each other's souls? What bearing of one another's burdens? What a mere jest is it, then, to talk so gravely of destroying what never was! The real truth is just the reverse of this: we introduce Christian fellowship where it was utterly destroyed. And the fruits of it have been peace, joy, love, and zeal for every good word and work." It is of great interest to trace the beginning of so important a change in the relation of Church members; to estimate its utility, its adaptation to the necessities of the untaught, untrained, and unspiritual. Who shall declare its value as a guard against the force of many temptations, of its opportunity for minute inquiry into the spiritual needs and perils of individual believers, for direct appeal to the conscience, for effective supervision, for control, and comfort, and guidance? It stirs the springs of brotherly affection; it unites in bonds of brotherly communion. It has its valuable social aspects, drawing many together, not merely in acts of neighbourly kindness, but in the ministries of profound spiritual intercourse. It calls into play an unconscious influence by which the watchfulness of friendship and the check of public observation restrain from many forms of evil. It creates or fosters the sense of common interest, the recognition of common rights, privileges, and duties. The feeling of fellowship and support makes the timid bold, and cheers the lonely and sad; while the assurance of sympathy encourages the faint under tribulation, and nerves the feeble for toil.

By its class-meetings Methodism affirms that Church membership is not perfected by sacramental ordinances; that, though baptism may be the divinely appointed initiatory rite, and the sacrament of the Lord's Supper the authorized sign and seal of abiding membership, yet there could be no perfecting of Church membership in the absence of a mutual ministry of edification—"that which every joint supplieth." It obviously believes, and thus explicitly declares, that "unto *each one* of us" is "grace given according to the measure of the gift of Christ;" and it affirms it to be the duty of each to use that gift, as far as opportunity permits, for the good of all. This carries a twofold idea— that of individual personal supervision; that of profound individual responsibility. Each is to come under care; each is to minister in his measure. Each is the object of solicitude and oversight; each must do his part, howsoever small, towards the general good. This mutual responsibility and mutual ministry of the members of the Church is a prime feature in the true idea of the class-meeting.[1]

It is the genius of Methodism not to deal merely with masses of people. It has seized upon the great truth of the necessity for a careful regard for each individual member of the Church. It is a ministry to the individual life. It makes the welfare of each the Church's solemn duty. Not only is each name recorded; every one is under weekly observation. The original rule remains, if the original practice is not always observed: "It is the business of the leader to see each person in his class once a week, at least." This attention to the individual, both in the initial stage of the religious life and in the course of its progress, has always been regarded as of the utmost importance; and equally the calling into play the talents of every member. Each is made a centre of influence; and though many may

[1] Appendix B.

have little ability, what there is is discovered, and no one is suffered to be wholly idle and lost. " The class-meeting, when rightly conducted, is a fountain of incalculable blessing. It is in the class-meeting that the young convert first tests his power to speak of the things of God. In the prayers and testimonies of the class meeting are to be found the first training of prayer leaders, mission workers, Sunday-school teachers, local preachers, and ministers. But for the practice of simple and fervent utterance in the class-meeting, it is very doubtful whether such a harvest of Christian workers as has been reaped, year by year, could ever have been grown or gathered amongst us." [1]

Thus the class-meeting answered at once the several ends of the oversight of individual members, the cultivation of the individual Christian character, the promotion of individual Christian service, the expansion of the individual religious experience. It made each answerable to the Church, and caused each to be nurtured by the Church. This was an original feature. It was designed to supply the lack, the inevitable lack, of ministerial service.

The Church thus becomes far less idealistic in its structure. It is a more real building. It is compacted together. The communion of saints is no longer a mere idealism: it is a reality. The Methodist view is that the full meaning of the κοινωνία, the apostolic "fellowship," of the early Church is not reached unless it include the mutual participation in the benefit of the gifts of each. That the Church should make provision for the exercise of the gifts of all " the saints," perfected "unto the work of ministering, unto the building up of the body of Christ," is strictly in harmony

[1] *Report of Committee on Church Membership, Min. Conference*, 1889, p. 406.

with the will of Him Who "gave" all "gifts unto men."[1] And if the Methodist plan be not in all respects the best, we will use it quietly until a better be proposed, not hesitating to say that there is not a more efficient means in use by the Christian Church at this day. Whether this particular form should be made obligatory upon all I will not presume to affirm.

It is not needful to suppose that the class-meeting is the only or the chief way of fulfilling the apostolic injunction; and let it be modestly confessed that the frequent lapses from the Methodist Society, and the apparent impossibility of making very great advances in respect of numbers, may point to its inapplicability to universal conditions. If, however, the class-meeting does not meet the necessities of all, or if it does not accord with the taste of all, and so fails to prove itself to be a means of spiritual fellowship adapted to all, it nevertheless meets the requirement of the most needy; it responds to a demand on the part of the penitent inquirer, the feeble in faith, the troubled, the timid, the doubtful, the young and uninstructed disciple. It has afforded abundant opportunity for succouring the immature, and for giving solace and comfort to the sorrowful; while it has secured the progressive culture of the Christian character to thousands upon thousands who but for it must have gone on in loneliness, lacking the reality of a true Christian communion, or any other than a merely idealistic fellowship with the visible Church of which they were members. If the Christian Church is a

---

[1] I wish to draw special attention to the clear, thorough, and very valuable teaching on this subject given by one of my predecessors in the lectureship, in *The Holy Catholic Church, the Communion of Saints*, by the Rev. Benjamin Gregory, D.D.

brotherhood, that brotherhood is best shown and promoted by mutual interest, sympathy, and help, by brotherly intercourse on those high subjects in which all have an equal participation. It is not necessary to affirm that Wesley was raised up in order to establish these wonderfully useful little meetings, although the introduction of them into the Church was a service of sufficient value to deserve for the originator not a little honour and distinction. But running through the institution is a thread of teaching which of itself raises Wesley's work to a high pitch of instructiveness and value—the idea of the mutual interest and mutual service of all the members of the Church; of careful, minute, individual oversight, defence, and instruction; the calling out of their several gifts for the benefit of all. It is the idea of brotherhood realized in brotherly communion, brotherly intercourse, and brotherly help. It responds to the exhortation—

"Let each his friendly aid afford,
And feel his brother's care."

This is the true brotherhood. Here, indeed, the rich and the poor meet together.

Some may be independent of the help which the class-meeting affords; they are thereby declared able to help them to whom it is a boon and a blessing. This is not the place in which to make an appeal, but the very mention of the fact that many are capable of rendering help to their more needy brethren in the faith, who nevertheless withhold that help, points to the great loss the Church sustains through the failure of such persons to use wisely and faithfully their gifts for the common good. This was and is the Methodist idea of Christian fellowship;

and it was part of its high calling—part of its essential mission—to reintroduce to the Churches this kind of Christian communion of mutual oversight and mutual service.

It is right here to point out one valuable result of the class-meeting, which made its appearance at a very early period. I refer to the calling into play to so large an extent of the gifts and endowments of the Church. It has laid an emphasis on the duty of every believer to do something, not only for the Church within, but for the community without. It lays on every one the responsibility of seeking to promote the welfare of others. The rules of the Society are explicit on this point. "It is expected of all who continue in these Societies that they should continue to evidence their desire for salvation, secondly, by doing good, by being in every kind merciful after their power; as they have opportunity, doing good of every possible sort, and as far as is possible, to all men."

It is a part of the calling and mission of Methodism to teach this, and the entire Church is indebted to it for giving prominence to this call of every believer to fulfil his own personal and individual mission. By the way in which it draws out and engages the direct service of every member of the Church according to his gift, his "measure of faith," Methodism has taught and trained an army of workers. Only those who are familiar with the class-meeting can understand how efficiently it serves the purpose of detecting the first evidences of spiritual endowment, and the opportunities it affords of developing the same. If Methodism has not devised all the methods by which Christian men are found to-day fulfilling their call to usefulness, it certainly drew the attention of the Churches to the precious treasure each may hold of undeveloped power, genius, grace, and ability. Methodism has no exclusive prerogative in this. Happily the Churches now widely share in the holy joy which prompts to active, self-denying service; but it has been a glory of Methodism from the beginning to call into use the abilities of the members of the Church, each with his psalm or doctrine or exhortation.

The utility of the Society fellowship has not escaped the observation of the thoughtful around, as the following testimonies will show.

Mr. Guinness Rogers writes: "Methodism has unquestionably laid hold of a grand idea in connection with the Church, and has worked it out with an ingenuity of tact, an intensity of feeling, a large-hearted devotion, and an unrelaxing diligence which are beyond all praise. A society thus welded together by the multitude of its common interests, as well as by the depth of its spiritual sympathies, naturally becomes a powerful organization. It is the glory of Methodism that it has a compact, well-disciplined, and mighty force always available for purposes of aggression. It has thus opportunities for prosecuting its work on which other bodies of Christians cannot look without feelings of admiration and of envy." [1]

It has been well asserted by the Rev. Dr. Dale, that, "For the protection and development of the Christian life, and the formation of the ideal Christian character, a Christian environment—a Christian Society—is necessary. The fellowship of the saints, with its ethical and spiritual traditions, with its spiritual brotherhood, and with its supernatural atmosphere, is a great means of grace."

[1] *Church Systems*, pp. 590, 591.

And he bears this testimony:—

"Methodism made one striking and original contribution to the institutions of the Church in the class-meeting. Never, so far as I know, in any Church has there been so near an approach to the ideal of pastoral oversight as the class-meeting, in its perfect form, provides; and it also provides for that communion of saints which is almost as necessary for the strength and the joy and the harmonious growth of the Christian life as fellowship with God."[1]

And again:—

"Methodism indeed owes very much of its enduring strength to those special institutions of which the class-meeting is the most conspicuous example, by which its members are permanently drawn into the most intimate religious relations with each other."[2]

"The perfecting here spoken of is chiefly the training of stunted powers or organs into their proper activity. It is a process of culture and development, but not with the man himself for its ideal end. Its end is 'a work of ministering,' some form of service to be rendered to others. For ministering is the one universal function of all 'saints,' all individual members of the Church, the common element in all functions."[3]

These fourfold elements are the essential and distinctive, characteristics of Methodism: they stand in the closest possible relation to each other. These are the four corner-stones of the Methodist building.

---

[1] *The Old Evangelicalism and the New*, pp. 31, 32.
[2] *Ibid.* pp. 17, 18.
[3] *The Sense and Service of Membership the Measure of true Soundness in the Body.* Dr. Hort.

CHAPTER II.

THE MISSION OF METHODISM DEFINED.

1. *The Development of the Idea of Methodism in the Mind of Wesley.*

I now propose to consider the gradual unfolding of the purpose for which Methodism was raised up, and the development of the idea of that purpose in the mind of Wesley and his coadjutors.

We see the little band of workers led forward by one constraining and overpowering motive. With an eager impetuosity they press on in the pursuit of their one design —the salvation of the ungodly. This is their one work; the work to which they believe they are called; and each man bends his energies to accomplish it. It is out of this work that Methodism grows. They do not lay down a plan and work towards it. It does not enter their minds to demand a plan, or to consider beforehand whereunto their work would lead. There is no attempt to formulate the purpose for which they were raised up. There is, at present, no system, no organization; all is tentative and experimental. The tree must attain to some measure of growth in its freedom, before the pruning-knife or the training hand can be laid upon it. We now can see all to have been unfolding naturally as from a central idea.

(1) There are distinct and clearly defined epochs in the early history of Methodism which it is well to observe. One of these lay in the first years after the "conversions," from 1738 to 1744, the year of the first Conference. During this period we watch the Wesleys absorbed in their devoted toil. At first they alternate between London and Bristol, and Bristol and Oxford; then they gradually extend their boundaries to places beyond, meeting one another occasionally, writing frequently. Through these years the work grows. They are, I think, years of great interest. The simplicity of the aim of the workers, the greatness of their labours, the faithfulness of their service, the astonishing effects of their preaching, and the extraordinary nature of many of the incidents that happened, all combine to invest the period with a most attractive character. It was distinguished by great evangelistic fervour, by fierce strife with rude opposing forces, and by many grave anxieties. In it grotesque effects of the great awakening upon the minds of some, and hallowed, peaceful, sacred effects upon the minds of others, who are brought out of darkness into marvellous light, were witnessed.

There was no Conference during this period. There was a sheepfold for the safety of the sheep, as they, scattered abroad and bleeding, are fetched back to be cared for, healed and fed; for the Society received its complete elaboration during these years.

It was during this period that the grand experiment of the open-air preaching was made, and the power of the gospel so wondrously demonstrated. It was while its chief actors, all moved by one impulse, all working from one inspiration, steadily pursued their one purpose, that the essential elements of the Methodism of the future began to develop themselves, long before there was any conception of a distinct community, or a more highly organized body than a simple Society forming a suitable means by which the good work could be both advanced and conserved, and by which the new believers could be built up in faith and godly discipline.

It was while engaged in this evangelistic toil that the conviction began to dawn upon Wesley that there was a distinct and definite call to himself and his co-workers and to the Society that clung to them. And the further he went with that work, the more clearly did it appear to him that the organization which was growing around them, as they with singleness of eye kept the one lofty aim before them, was destined of God to accomplish a great purpose in the world—the purpose for which Methodism was raised up, which constitutes the mission of Methodism, and which ultimately so defined itself to him.

I cannot help repeating that it was whilst they were pursuing their one object, and adapting their methods to the necessities of the hour, that Methodism developed, as it was needed. And we must see this development taking place particularly around Wesley, and see how, concurrently, the idea formed itself in his mind until it assumed a very definite shape.

Soon after the commencement of the field-preaching, he tells us that he had many thoughts concerning the unusual manner of his ministering, which he says he frequently laid before the Lord; and carefully weighed whatever objections he heard against it. His sentiments are expressed in a letter addressed to a friend, from which the following extracts are made :—

"If you ask on what principle, then, I acted: It was this: 'a desire to be a Christian; and a conviction that whatever I judge conducive thereto, that I am bound to do; wherever I judge I can best answer this end, thither it is my duty to go.' On this principle I set out for America; on this, I visited the Moravian Church; and on the same am I ready now (God being my helper) to go to Abyssinia or China, or whithersoever it shall please God, by this conviction, to call me."

"But, in the meantime, you think I ought to sit still, because otherwise I should invade another's office if I interfered with other people's business, and intermeddled with souls that did not belong to me. You accordingly ask, 'How is it that I assemble Christians who are none of my charge, to sing psalms, and pray, and hear the Scriptures expounded? and think it hard to justify doing this in other men's parishes, upon Catholic principles.' . . . They weigh nothing with me. I allow no other rule, whether of faith or practice, than the Holy Scriptures. But on scriptural principles, I do not think it hard to justify whatever I do. God in Scripture commands me, according to my power, to instruct the ignorant, reform the wicked, confirm the virtuous. Man forbids me to do this in another's parish— that is, in effect, to do it at all, seeing I have now no parish of my own, nor probably ever shall. Whom then shall I hear, God or man? 'If it be just to obey man rather than God, judge you. A dispensation of the gospel is committed to me, and woe is me if I preach not the gospel.' But where shall I preach it, upon the principles you mention? Why, not in Europe, Asia, Africa, or America; not in any of the Christian parts, at least, of the habitable earth. For all these are, after a sort, divided into parishes."

"Suffer me now to tell you my principles in this matter. I look upon all the world as my parish; thus far I mean, that, in whatever part of it I am, I judge it meet, right, and my bounden duty to declare unto all that are willing to hear, the glad tidings of salvation. This is the work which I know God has called me to; and sure I am that His blessing attends it. Great encouragement have I, therefore, to be faithful in fulfilling the work He hath given me to do. His servant I am, and, as such, am employed according to the plain direction of His word, 'As I have opportunity, doing good unto all men.' And His providence clearly concurs with His word; which has disengaged me from all things else, that I might singly attend on this very thing, 'and go about doing good.'"[1]

This was in 1739. Thus early was he confronted with the demand for a justification of his procedure. So methodical a thinker, so logical a reasoner, and one so much accustomed to obey rule, must sooner or later question himself; and thus he declares the principles by which he is guided, and the motives by which he is actuated. There is no setting this aside. A man with such a conviction is not to be easily controlled by any authority that has not its seat in his own convictions, for the alternative is instantly suggested, "Whom then shall I hear, God or man?"

This was his point of departure from Church order as it

[1] *Works*, vol. i. pp. 200-2.

was generally expounded. Has he justified that departure? We must seek an answer in his convictions, and the scriptural authority by which he supported them; in the condition of surrounding society; in the necessities of the people; in the supineness and inefficiency of the clergy at the time; and in the wonderful effects of his labours.

If Wesley's work needs justifying, that justification is certainly furnished by the history of the National Church in the last century; by the imperative demand for such a work as this, if the nation was to be saved from utter demoralization, if not from anarchy and civil rebellion; and by the great results that have followed that work,—results which have so extended themselves that they are to be found tinging the present aspects of Christianity in all parts of the world. With a consensus of judgment that work is held to have been as effective in awakening religious life in the country as it was rendered necessary by the indolence or apathy of the Churches and the deep degeneracy of the national morals and manners.

We must carefully discriminate between the work which Wesley felt himself bound to do—the one work of preaching the gospel and caring for the souls of men—and the formation of any organized plan which could by any means be supposed likely to develop into a Church. In the years we are now considering, which I have distinguished as constituting the first epoch, there was not, as we have seen, so much as a Conference. The work had greatly extended when Wesley felt it needful to sit down with his fellow-workers to consider any controlling principles for his own guidance, or for the direction of those around him. There were about forty lay preachers.

Societies had been formed in many parts of the country, and several thousands of members had been gathered into them—in London alone probably near 2000. Persecution had been roused to a violent pitch. A small number of clergymen had thrown in their lot with the little band of Methodists. Alas! the following had withdrawn— Ingham, Hervey, Hall, Gambold, Hutchins, Stonehouse, and Cennick.

It was in this period that the great innovation, the *lay-preaching*, was commenced. Wesley did not initiate it. It was done before he was aware, and without his approval. But it soon received his sanction, and through that sanction it speedily became an established, as it has always been an honoured, institution of Methodism. Wesley wrote very forcibly in its defence.

After the first experiments of the field-preaching had been made, and the idea of the Society had been fully developed, Wesley took his first evangelistic journeys beyond the limits of London, Oxford, and Bristol—the first foci of the movement. Thus another phase of the expansive evangelism was entered upon. He had begun to use the freedom expressed in his significant watchword, "I look upon the world as my parish."[1]

But there is another feature of the work to which prominence must be given. It was in these first years that Charles Wesley, "the bard of Methodism," made some of his earliest and best contributions to the Church's psalter. He began to sing on the day of his conversion; and he sang "the hymn" still louder when his brother

---
[1] A brief but interesting summary of the progress of Methodism in these first years is given in Smith's *History of Methodism*, vol. i. pp. 191-209.

was brought to him rejoicing, saying, "I believe, I believe."

The awakening of the religious life in that gifted man called all his powers into activity. As in the Lutheran Reformation in Germany, and the Nonconformist in our own land, so here the awakened Christian sentiment found its natural expression in song.

During the time of which I am speaking several books of hymns and one of tunes were issued. Two small volumes had already been published by John Wesley, one in Charlestown and one in London. They were compilations, and the rich evangelical Wesleyan element of subsequent publications was wanting in them. They were published before the "conversion." Charles had issued nothing as yet. But in 1739 the first edition of "Hymns and Sacred Poems" appeared, four editions of which were published in four years. In the following year (1740) another volume bearing the same title, but a different work, appeared. It was afterwards incorporated with the former. The next year, 1741, "A Collection of Psalms and Hymns" was published by John Wesley, which had passed into three editions in 1744. This was in use fifty years ago in chapels where the morning liturgy was used, and was called the "Morning Hymn-Book." In the same year (1741) two separate and interesting issues appeared, entitled "Hymns on God's Everlasting Love," and in the following year (1742) a third book bearing the title "Hymns and Sacred Poems," also "A Collection of Tunes," and a small selection of hymns for the benefit of the poor, issued at threepence. In 1744 "A Collection of Moral and Sacred Poems from the most celebrated

English Authors" showed the value which Wesley placed on poetical writings; whilst a small collection of "Funeral Hymns" bore testimony to the strength of faith and joyfulness of hope with which the first Methodists were encouraged to meet death, and furnished an earnest of the many and precious songs of exultation for the happy deathbeds witnessed throughout the land since the revival.

In examining these books, one is struck by the greatness of the gift vouchsafed by the Giver of all good gifts, both to the writers, and through them to the Church at large. That the revival, promoted by the preaching of John Wesley, was aided in a very large degree by the hymns which Charles Wesley sang, has become a widespread conviction, which I have no wish to disturb. Charles Wesley carried conviction to the hearts of thousands, and published to them the gospel of peace on the gentler wings of sacred song, and stimulated their love and their devotion, and expanded their views of the Christian life, brightening their hope, confirming their faith, and wooing them into the rich fields of an ample Christian experience.

These are the distinguishing features of the first epoch named by me.

(2) It is interesting to notice how slowly the great idea of Methodism presented itself to Wesley's mind, though he, more than any of his colleagues, was able to interpret it; for he was not only in the midst of the work, he was its very centre, its ruling spirit. Only gradually, however, could he discern the providential purpose, although from the beginning he had at times been compelled to

consider whither his work was tending him. But it was by slow steps, as that work itself advanced, that he was led to form a definite idea of the calling—the mission of Methodism. It was sufficient for him and for his fellow-labourers for a considerable time to see that the preaching of the gospel was effective, that multitudes were turned from the power of Satan to serve the living God, as he would have said truly, turned from hell to heaven. And it was enough for him that he could gather them into the home and fellowship of the Societies, where they could be guarded and encouraged, and screened from evil. No other mission was desired by him or his co-labourers than this, and we have seen how these first years had been expended upon it.

But now the time had arrived when the necessities of the Societies and of the work generally seemed to demand a more careful consideration of principles and of modes of action. With this in view, a series of Conferences was held during the next five years, another period of equal definiteness with the former.

The record of the proceedings of these early "conversations" is comprised in what are called the "Doctrinal and Disciplinary Minutes." This is a first and separate series of "Minutes." They form the basis of all subsequent Methodism. During the following fifteen years no annual Minutes were published; but in the year 1753 or 1757 the first edition of the so-called "Large Minutes" was issued, it being a compendium of what had been discussed in 1749 and the five previous Conferences.

In regard to the summoning of the first Conference Wesley tells us that he wrote to several clergymen, and to all who then "served" him "as sons in the gospel," desiring them to meet him in London, to give him their advice concerning the best method of carrying on "the work of God"—a phrase very frequently employed by him, and an appropriate term to represent the incipient Methodism, as indeed it is, or ought to be, to represent all Methodism. The Conference was begun at the Foundery on Monday the 25th day of June, 1744, and it continued five days. The following persons were present:—John Wesley, Charles Wesley, John Hodges, the Rector of Wenvo; Henry Piers, Vicar of Bexley; Samuel Taylor, Vicar of Quinton; and John Meriton. It was first inquired, Whether any of the "Lay Brethren" should be present at the Conference; and it was agreed to invite, from time to time, such of them as they should judge proper. On that day Thomas Richards, Thomas Maxfield, John Bennet, and John Downes "were accordingly brought in."

This is the germ of what has become a great and powerful organization, the largest and most compact ecclesiastical administrative body in the world.

Throughout these Conferences the following principles were carefully observed:—(1) The absolute supremacy of the Scriptures as the final appeal in all things; (2) The responsibility of private judgment, and the independence of individual conviction. The little company, after spending some time in prayer, considered, "What to teach, how to teach, and what to do,—*i.e.* How to regulate our doctrine, discipline, and practice." Here is the future organization in embryo.

In the consideration of the first question, "What to

teach," they make the first formulated statements of Methodist doctrine. What do those statements embrace? First and foremost, as was most meet, is the cardinal doctrine, the very foundation-stone of this still standing Church, justification by faith, with its concomitants, never more sharply and succinctly defined. They describe the needed preliminary repentance, and works meet for repentance, the nature of saving faith, the consciousness of salvation by the witness of the Holy Spirit, the necessity for godly living in order to final salvation, the doctrine of Christian perfection and the universal fall, together with guards against Calvinism and Antinomianism, in the face of which Methodism stood. With what crystalline clearness are these subjects defined! With what keenness of search do these men interrogate! With what precision do they reply! I venture to say that no equal number of lines in any theological writing contain a teaching of more exquisite exactness, combined with an equally ample expansion and carefully balanced statements, than is presented in this unique catechetical document.

All these doctrines—essentially practical doctrines—are such as we should expect a handful of reformers to use as weapons. To these they confine themselves. Where did they learn them? The answer is plain. They learnt them from the best writers of their Church—the Church of the Reformation; and they proved them to themselves in the depths of their own experience, and, in debate, by appeals to the Holy Scripture as the one standard of authority, and to the Articles and Homilies, as the doctrines of the Church in full agreement with the Scriptures.

These are the doctrinal truths which it was the original,

the especial calling of Methodism to rescue from oblivion, to proclaim to the Churches, to urge upon the attention of a careless public, to promulgate and defend by its teaching, to illustrate by its living. That is the calling of Methodism still, and none the less so because happily so many of the Churches to-day join hand in hand in this work.

These doctrines were all or in part reconsidered in each of the following Conferences.

But we must observe that, while Wesley and his little band of helpers were thus early laying a sound doctrinal basis as the very foundation of Methodism, they were none the less careful in laying also the foundation of a religious Society.

One of the first works they attempt is to determine their relation to the Church of England. They claim for themselves acknowledgment as true sons of the Church, and they justify their claim. Guided by Articles 20 and 26, they define a member of the Church of England as "a believer hearing the pure word of God preached, and partaking of the sacraments duly administered within that Church." Perhaps a side reproof is here intended to men who did not preach "the pure word," and an admonition to those who, therefore, did not hear the pure word; and reproof and admonition both to the many who, calling themselves Churchmen, did not partake of the sacraments themselves, and would fain excise those who did.

But it seems most probable that this carefulness of definition at the beginning was designed by the members of the Conference to prove their own right to be considered within the Church's fellowship; to show that they did not, as they were accused of doing, separate themselves from the Church, even by what seemed to be very unwarrantable methods of procedure, or encourage others to do so. They are able to answer the direct question, "Do we separate from the Church?" by the clear answer, "We conceive not. We hold communion therewith for conscience' sake by constantly attending both the word preached and the sacraments administered therein."

Turning aside to consider the possibility of their entailing schism upon their hearers either then or afterwards, their early and prescient reply is that their followers will remain in the Church unless they be thrust out, and that in their judgment they will be either thrust out or will leaven the Church. But they declare that they cannot neglect present duty from any fear of future consequences for which they cannot hold themselves responsible. They subsequently (1747) return to this question of schism, and, examining the scriptural use of the word, affirm its only meaning to be "a causeless breach, rupture, or division made among the members of Christ, among those who are the living body of Christ, and members in particular."[1] Of this they declare themselves to be no more guilty "than of rebellion or murder."

They further declare themselves to be willing to obey the will of bishops in all things indifferent and in harmony with the canons of the Church, as far as they can with a safe conscience. This supremacy of conscience is the cementing bond of the stones in the foundations of

---

[1] The "Minutes" say, "The word occurs only twice in the New Testament." The passages referred to are 1 Cor. i. 10 (margin) and 1 Cor. xii. 25. But the word occurs also in the Authorized Version of 1 Cor. xi. 18, and in five other verses in the original. In all these places it means a "breach, rupture, or division."

Methodism. More than once it is reaffirmed, thus establishing a principle already enunciated by them, that each was free, for each was responsible. This is a firm, bold, calm stand within their rights as members of the Church, and a clear affirmation of their purposes respecting that membership. It was their first utterance; they never departed from it.

Then points of discipline were considered, a first question being, "How are the people divided who desire to be under your care?" This is the primary and simple idea of the religious association they are forming. We read of united societies, bands, select societies, and penitents, with their several definitions, rules, and officers.[1] They have "ministers," who are clergymen, and "assistants," who are lay assistants, "allowable only in cases of necessity." They have also "stewards, leaders of bands, leaders of classes, visitors of the sick, schoolmasters, and housekeepers." It is a very definite organization, but it all clusters around the word "Society."

They put and answer the following questions:—"What is the office of a minister?" "What is it to be moved by the Holy Ghost to take this office upon yourself?" "Is field-preaching unlawful?" "What is the best general method of preaching?" "Where should we endeavour to preach most?" The answer to which is, "Where we can preach in the church." They justify field-preaching as not "contrary to any law human or divine;" but "to avoid offence," they will "never preach *without* doors when they can with conveniency preach *within*." They also judge it advisable to extend their work "a little and little

[1] Rules for the penitents, if ever formed, have not been preserved.

farther from London, Bristol, St. Ives, Newcastle, or any other Society. So a little leaven would spread with more effect and less noise ;" this being the best way of spreading the gospel, which is their one aim.

In the following year (1745) they review their work, and again consider "points of discipline," when Wesley more fully declares his principles of Church government. The axe is laid to the root of the trees; and by one stroke he cuts at, if not through, the apostolical succession theory. "Can he be a spiritual governor of the Church who is not a believer, not a member of it?"

To the Rubrics they are willing to submit, but not to the mere will of any governor, temporal or spiritual. "Therefore," says Wesley, "if any bishop wills that I should not preach the gospel, his will is no law to me." And even if a law be produced against the preaching, the answer is, "I am to obey God rather than man"—a far-reaching answer, as we know, in these days.

The important question is then proposed, "Is Episcopal, Presbyterian, or Independent Church government most agreeable to reason?" They do not say, to Scripture. Why, was afterwards to appear.

The answer issues in the approval of a modified Episcopalianism—a union of congregations, independent of one another, but not independent of a common head, or pastor, or bishop, or overseer.

The relation between pastor and flock is determined to be one of mutual consent only. They confess themselves compelled to take a more decided stand against the opposing clergy, and they resolve to extend their evangelistic labours to every town where there is an open door; and even to make a trial, in Cornwall and Wales, of preaching without "settling any Societies,"—a determination which, after trial, they found it needful to abandon; for, say they, "We have preached for more than a year without forming Societies in a large tract of land, from Newcastle to Berwick-on-Tweed, and almost all the seed has fallen by the wayside. There is scarce any fruit of it remaining."

In the following year (1746) they add to these views the decision that a congregation has power to choose its own pastor. They define an apostle to be "one sent to convert the heathen;" a prophet to be "a builder up of the faithful." And then the important question is suggested, "In what view are we and our helpers to be considered?" and the significant answer is given, "Perhaps as extraordinary messengers designed of God to provoke the others to jealousy." This was the first time that they proposed the question to themselves. The clear and full definition of the divine purpose in raising them up does not appear to have been reached before the first revision of the Large Minutes in the year 1763: six or seven years after the first edition was issued.

They then introduce the three tests, ever afterwards applied, by which they propose to prove those "who believe they are moved by the Holy Ghost and called of God to preach." Have they grace and gifts and the divine seal—success? and they conclude, "As long as these three marks undeniably concur in any, we allow him to be called of God to preach." "These we receive," they say, "as sufficient evidence that he is moved thereto by the Holy Ghost." Who can tell the importance of this decision on the future development of the great revival? It is in harmony with all its fundamental principles; nay, it is one of them. If the whole work of Methodism is to be looked upon as a direct divine interposition, the calling and qualification of each of its servants must be " of God." To this hour the Methodist Conference has striven to be faithful to this principle.

Turning to our record again, we find the utmost caution is used to prevent mistakes in their judgment of the evidences of a divine call; and then they explain the avoidance of " more form and solemnity " in their method of " receiving a new labourer," on the ground that " there is something of stateliness in it," and because they would " not make haste ; " for they " desire barely to follow Providence as it gradually opens."

Passing by some minor points, we find them justifying the extension of their work beyond parish and all other boundaries, by judging that a call of Providence is to be found in—" 1. An invitation from some one that is worthy; from a serious man, fearing God, who has a house to receive us; 2. A probability of doing more good by going thither than by staying longer where we are ; " and they resolve " to send more labourers " into parts where it is observable that " God is pleased to pour out His Spirit more abundantly."

In the following year (1747) they resolve fearlessly to re-examine their former decisions, assured that if their first principles are true, they will bear the strictest investigation; and if false, the sooner they are overturned the better; and they encourage one another to pray for a " willingness to receive light; an invariable desire to know of every doctrine whether it be of God ; " and then they probe to the heart's core with this searching question, "How far does each of us agree to submit to the unanimous judgment of the rest?" and it is answered, "In speculative things each can only submit so far as his judgment shall be convinced. In every practical point, so far as we can without wounding our several consciences." They then ask, "Can a Christian submit any farther than this to any man, or number of men, upon earth?" and they lay down a broad principle in these earnest words, by which they reply to the question: "It is undeniably plain he cannot: either to Pope, Council, Bishop, or Convocation. And this is that grand principle of every man's right to private judgment, in opposition to implicit faith in man, on which Calvin, Luther, Melancthon, and all the ancient Reformers, both at home and abroad, proceeded: 'Every man must think for himself; since every man must give an account of himself to God.'"

The question of their obedience to the governors and rulers of the Church is thoroughly debated and answered. "Upon what principle do you act, while you sometimes obey and sometimes not?" The answer is, "It is entirely consistent. We act at all times on one plain, uniform principle: 'We will obey the rulers and the governors of the Church, whenever we can consistent with our duty to God; whenever we cannot, we will quietly obey God rather than man.'"

They go on to affirm that the Scriptures apply the word "Church" to "a single congregation;" and that there is no known instance or ground in the New Testament for a National Church. They believe the three orders of bishops, priests, and deacons to be "plainly described in the New Testament," and that they generally obtained in the early

Church; but they are not assured that God designed the same should obtain exclusively in all Churches in all ages. For they ask, "If this plan were essential to a Christian Church, what must become of all the foreign Reformed Churches?" "It would follow they are no parts of the Church of Christ! a consequence full of shocking absurdity." And they conclude there must "in the nature of things be numberless accidental varieties in the government of various Churches. For as God variously dispenses His gifts of nature, providence, and grace, both the offices themselves and the officers in each ought to be varied from time to time;" and they further declare that the reason why there is "no determinate plan of Church government appointed in Scripture," is "because the wisdom of God had a regard to this necessary variety."

In these conversations there is an apparent mixing up of what some might think ought to have been kept separate. The "Society" seems to be treated as though it were a Church, or designed to become one. It has its "ministers," whose duty it is "to watch over the souls whom God commits to their charge, as they who must give account," which ministers must be "moved by the Holy Ghost to take upon themselves this office." In the absence of the "minister" it is the duty of an "assistant" to "feed and guide, to teach and govern the flock." For said "assistants" rules are drawn up which to-day are judged worthy to be guides to all the Methodist ministers, and are regularly read at their annual meetings.

Although they are considering only the best ways of guarding their Societies, and with no, even hidden, purpose of separating from the Church or founding a new sect, they do nevertheless lay the basis on which the subsequent structure of the Methodist Churches came to be built. It is very remarkable that Wesley and his friends should at so early a period of their work have felt themselves called upon to consider the very bases of Church organization. We have only one explanation to give for this. It is evident that the constitution of the "Society" did not require it; and the framers of that Society assuredly had no idea of forming a Church of any kind, much less one differing from the Church of England. Yet they carefully and minutely debated in these first Conferences the very foundations of Church organization and government. My explanation is, that Wesley felt the irresistible pressure of his one work urging him on independently of Church authorities, if not even in opposition to them; and at the same time he felt himself constrained to find a justification for the anomalous position which he was compelled to occupy. I think it is obvious that most of the discussions at these early Conferences of what were really the fundamental principles of Church organization were necessitated by the peculiar, if not irregular, position in which these men were placed. Here were clergymen having no benefice, going through the country preaching and even encouraging laymen to do the same, sometimes forbidden by the minister of the parish, sometimes even by the bishop of the diocese. If they judged their position to be legal, others did not; and they were in the difficulty of having to justify their conduct first to themselves and then to the public. It was on this account that they searched matters to the bottom. It certainly was with no intention of forming a Church; although, when the days came which they did not foresee, the foundations were found to have been laid, broadly, firmly, compactly, on which Methodism, as a Church structure, could be built.

They were dealing with what they called a "Society," or a union of Societies, not a Church. But they applied their ecclesiastical principles to this Society, and thus unconsciously placed it upon a Church basis. I say unconsciously, for it could not have been their purpose at that early period to make provision for the Society developing into a Church, nor could it have been their expectation at that time that it would ever do so.

We must therefore not suppose that the discussions on Church organization which occupied the first five Conferences were held with a view to found a Church. They were held in order to enable these men to search the very ground on which they built up their own work. They acknowledged a divine call. It was supreme with them; and they acknowledged the existence of a Church in the land —a Church to which they belonged, to which they clung. How far were the officers of that Church to be the interpreters to them of that call? It was evident to them that their opponents were not competent judges either of their work or of their call to that work. They knew that if bishop and parish priest had the true spirit, they would not hinder but help the work. They believed that they had a commission higher than any dignitary could confer. Moreover, they had been regularly constituted ministers of the Church. They heard the word as it was preached in the Church and communicated with strict regularity. They did not permit their irregular services to interfere with the regular services of the Church. For many years no service was allowed in Church hours; and their services were always acknowledged to be additional to those of the Church, not substitutionary. This answered the complaint that they separated from the Church, or opposed it. But they had a commission to preach, an inward conviction of duty: they had due qualifications, an authoritative recognition. Armed with these, they went forth. Who could gainsay them?

It was here they recognised their mission—the mission of Methodism in its earlier stages of development. They judged themselves to be " extraordinary messengers," what would in our day be called " missioners ; " and with this additional feature, that they were perhaps sent to provoke others to jealousy. We see them then urged on by their one great impulse, and being brought by it into collision with unsympathizing clergy and even opposing bishops. This it was which led to the careful examination of their position. They dared not go back or cease their cry to their ungodly, sorrowful, perishing neighbours. They would reach them by a faithful and decorous observance of Church order if possible; but if that order prevented, it must give way. The powerful spirit within them brooked no resistance. Church order if possible; but if that impeded, Providence would use it (as Wesley said it did) to "thrust them out." Nothing else could satisfy this strongest yearning of their hearts. " Woe is me," cried one and another, "if I preach not the gospel."

It was not to gratify a love of popularity, or a passion to appear before the public. Wesley affirmed he would rather take pupils at Oxford. It was an irresistible compulsion—

"against my will." This was their exact conviction—their one controlling idea—"designed of God."

They did not enter upon this work by preference, or by arrangement. They were "raised up," "thrust out," constrained. It was not a Church arrangement, but a divine commission—the purpose of Divine Providence—an authoritative divine call. For the Churches it was an interposition, a divine work. This was the high ground they took—"God thrust us out, my brother and I, against our will, to raise up a holy people."[1] Wesley strove hard to keep within the lines of Church order; but there was something in his view of far higher moment than Church order. "Our calling is to save that which was lost." In pursuance of this great work, they came, as I have said, into collision with parish priest and unsympathizing bishop. The priest denied them the use of the pulpit, even forbade them to trespass on the parish boundaries to gather people to read and sing and pray. What must be done? The principle already determined upon is put into practice. They will obey their spiritual rulers in all things indifferent. But if bishop or priest or word of canon stand before them, they have but one answer, "Whom shall I hear, God or man?"

The distinctive mission of Methodism rises more clearly into view in their decisions on the necessity for the wider extension of the "field-preaching." The necessity arising as they affirm—"1. Because our calling is to save that which is lost. Now we cannot expect the wanderers from God to seek us. It is our part to go and seek them. 2. Because we are more peculiarly called, by going out into the highways and hedges (which none will do, if we do not) to

---

[1] *Minutes of Conference.*

compel them to come in. 3. Because that reason against it is not good, 'The house will hold all that come.' The house may hold all that will come to the house, but not all that would come to the field. 4. Because we have always found a greater blessing in field-preaching than in any other preaching whatever." This was in 1747. From all this it follows most plainly that, in the view of the earliest Methodists (the makers and founders of Methodism), it was their calling and mission to go out to seek the wanderers, those whom the Church did not attract, and neither reached nor sought to reach, the neglected, the outcasts—alas ! "the lost." This was none the less the case because they gave good heed to the Societies—the sheepfold into which were gathered the sheep from the wilderness ; for this was a part of the process of saving. But Methodism could not then, it cannot now, it never will, fulfil its mission without a supreme regard for the ungodly. Whatever may be said of Church training, of spiritual culture, or of the many Church activities, the central idea of the mission of Methodism is *to save the lost.*

These principles guided them to the end. Looking back towards the close of his life, Wesley makes the following entry in his *Journal:*—"One of the most important points considered at this Conference, was that of leaving the Church. The sum of a long conversation was— 1. That in a course of fifty years we had neither premeditately nor willingly varied from it in one article, either of doctrine or discipline. 2. That we were not yet conscious of varying from it in any point of doctrine. 3. That we have in a course of years, out of necessity, not choice, slowly and warily varied in some points of discipline, by preaching in the fields, by extemporary prayer, by employing lay preachers, by forming and regulating Societies, and by holding yearly Conferences. But we did none of these things till we were convinced we could no longer omit them, but at the peril of our souls."[1] This was the state of things at the close of the second epoch.

(3) Working upon these principles they go forward, indifferent as to what the work will ultimately grow. That they leave to the same Providence which, as they believe, had raised them up. To their minds there was, as yet, no mission beyond this. The idea of the mission of Methodism had not yet developed itself. It was not in their language a mission of Methodism at all; but simply, "In what way can we and our helpers—we, a few clergymen of the Church of England, and a few laymen who have consented to help us—be most useful?" It would be vain to seek a definition of the mission of Methodism yet. It may be preparing. Indeed it was, but the perfect idea was not reached until afterwards.

In viewing their work from a distance, we must, I think, see these men to be sustained by three simple but great principles, viz. a divine conviction; the seal of the divine testimony to the divine origin of that conviction; and the outward guidance of the Divine Providence. In these they firmly believed. The conviction is that they are called to preach. They have heard the authoritative command, "Go preach the gospel." It is the repetition of the original commission, given to the earliest apostles of "the faith," and ever repeated within the hearing of the called and faithful in the Church of God, and now given by the same

[1] Aug. 4, 1788.

One Master and Lord to disciples who are in the true succession of the obedient servants of His will. The seal of testimony to the divine origin of that call is to be found in the changed lives of the people. In these they exult as the true seals to their ministry; and (with just sufficient to meet their daily recurring and simple wants) these make up the ample hire they crave. These are their joy and rejoicing. And if they see that they are carrying on the work begun by apostles and prophets, it is no wonder that they apply prophetic terms to that work, or believe that the same Divine Lord "raised them up" that raised up the greater toilers of olden time.

The providential circumstances were found in that "thrusting out," by the closed doors of the Churches, which compelled them to go to the needy; in the singular fitness of their message to meet the spiritual demands of the people; and in the opening of their way from step to step, and from day to day.

It may be plainly seen that the conviction that God had "raised up" the Methodists for definite ends was slowly gaining firm hold of their minds, though what those ends were they did not fully define to themselves until a later date.

Then follow sixteen years of work, the records of which are supplied in the journals, the biographies, and the histories of Methodism which happily abound.

Of the Conferences of these years, as I have said, we have no published Minutes, beyond a sentence each year in Mr. Wesley's *Journal*. It is therefore impossible to tell how far matters were discussed. They were years of work, during which the number of ministers and helpers rose to 95. In two years afterwards (the first in which we have exact reports of numbers) there were 25,911 members in the Society.

In viewing the course of these years the one subject that claims our attention is the opinion still entertained on the question of the relation of Methodism to the Church. In the year 1755, three days were spent in considering the question, "Whether we ought to separate from the Church." Whatever was advanced on one side or the other (we are told) was seriously and calmly considered; and on the third day "we were all fully agreed in that general conclusion—that (whether it was *lawful* or not) it was no ways *expedient*." [1]

Again, in the following year, fifty of the preachers being met, they "largely considered the necessity of keeping in the Church and using the clergy with tenderness. And there was no dissenting voice." Wesley says, "God gave us all to be of one mind and of one judgment." And he adds, "My brother and I closed the Conference by a solemn declaration of our purpose never to separate from the Church; and all our brethren concurred therein."

Again, in the last of this series of Conferences (1764) he says: "The great point I now laboured for was a good understanding with all our brethren of the clergy who are heartily engaged in propagating vital religion." [2]

Two years afterwards (1766) the position of the Methodists in relation to the Church is again debated in reply to

---

[1] *Journal*, May 6, 1755.

[2] From the following year the "Minutes" were published with regularity. To the time of Mr. Wesley's death they were generally sold at one penny each, and were called "The Penny Minutes." The "Large Minutes,' a compilation from these, was a threepenny pamphlet.

the question, "Are we not then Dissenters?" They acknowledge, "We are irregular—1. By calling sinners to repentance in all places of God's dominion; 2. By frequently using extemporary prayer." But they stoutly affirm themselves to be "neither Dissenters nor Seceders." And they show cause; adding, "As we are not Dissenters from the Church now, so we will do nothing willingly which tends to a separation from it." They further declare their own brief service did not, and should not, supersede the service in the Church. Two years further on, the idea of a separated ministry had thoroughly taken hold of Wesley's mind.[1]

The Conference of the year 1769 marks a very definite period in the history, beyond which it is not necessary for me to pursue any minute investigations. By this time we are led to see that Wesley's attention was being turned towards the question of the future of Methodism. He read a paper to the assembled preachers, in which he says that he had tried to persuade the clergy of the land, who believed and preached salvation by faith, cordially to agree and not to hinder but help one another; that he had pressed it in private conversation, and then had written to fifty or sixty, but that only three vouchsafed an answer; so he had given it up. Turning to his own preachers, he said, "But it is otherwise with you, the travelling preachers in our Connexion. You are at present one body. You act in concert with each other, and by united counsels. And now is the time to consider what can be done in order to continue this union. Indeed," he adds, "as long as I live

---

[1] At the Conference of 1768 it was decided that the itinerant preachers should not follow trades. Some portions of the Minutes of these years are of great interest, especially as showing the condition of Methodism at the time.

there will be no great difficulty; I am under God a centre of union to all our travelling as well as local preachers. . . . But by what means may this connexion be preserved when God removes me from you?" He points to the probabilities of some procuring preferment in the Church —"perhaps a fourth of the whole number"—and of others turning Independents, and having separate congregations. He then sketched the outline of a plan for the continuance of this union after his death, and laid it before the Conference.[1] It was then suggested that, with a view to lay "a foundation for this future union," all who were willing should sign the following articles of agreement:—
" I. To devote ourselves entirely to God; denying ourselves, taking up our cross daily; steadily aiming at one thing, to save our own souls and them that hear us. II. To preach the old Methodist doctrines, and no other, contained in the Minutes of the Conferences. III. To observe and enforce the whole Methodist discipline laid down in the said Minutes." This was afterwards done, and the signatures were published in the Minutes for 1773, 4, and 5. This was the first decisive step towards providing for the perpetuation of Methodism.

At a very early period Wesley, ever given carefully to

---

[1] The following is the plan:—
"On notice of my death, let all the preachers in England and Ireland repair to London within six weeks; let them seek God by solemn fasting and prayer; let them draw up articles of agreement, to be signed by those who choose to act in concert; let those be dismissed who do not choose it, in the most friendly manner possible; let them choose by votes a committee of three, five, or seven, each of whom is to be moderator in his turn; let the committee do what I do now,—propose preachers to be tried, admitted, or excluded; fix the place of each preacher for the ensuing year, and the time of the next Conference."—(*Min. Conf.*, 1769.)

examine his steps, was led to inquire into the probable design of God in raising up the Methodist preachers. As early as the third Conference (1746) the question was proposed, "In what view are we and our helpers to be considered?" The reply was, "Perhaps as extraordinary messengers designed of God to provoke the others to jealousy." This was the first determinate statement on this subject. This is repeated in each issue of the "Large Minutes" until 1780, when it was stated with more definiteness to be "perhaps as extraordinary messengers (*i.e.* out of the ordinary way) designed (1) To provoke the regular ministers to jealousy; (2) To supply their lack of service toward those who are perishing for want of knowledge." [1]

In the year 1763, when it had become evident to Wesley and his "helpers" that a great work was opening before them, the first of a series of revisions of these "Minutes," under Wesley's hand, was made. This additional inquiry was inserted, "What may we reasonably believe to be God's design in raising up the preachers called Methodists?" The reply is, "To reform the nation, and, in particular, the Church; to spread scriptural holiness over the land." These words were repeated in each subsequent edition of the "Minutes" until the sixth, issued in 1789, when the significant words were prefixed, "Not to form any new sect." That was Wesley's writing two years before his death. These words, like the addition to the former sentence quoted above, indicate but too clearly Wesley's view of the tendency of affairs.

[1] In 1789 was added the reflection, "But how hard is it to abide here! Who does not wish to be a little higher? Suppose, to be ordained!"

Here then we have the final and complete definition of the mission of Methodism as apprehended by Wesley himself, and as approved by all his "helpers," to every one of whom was given a copy of the so-called "Large Minutes," having the words inscribed, "As long as you freely consent to, and earnestly endeavour to walk by, these rules, we shall rejoice to acknowledge you as a fellow-labourer." The work to which these men believed themselves to be called was extraordinary and irregular — "out of the ordinary way;" it was designed to be provocative of greater zeal and activity on the part of the clergy; to supply their lack of service to the neglected portions of the population; to aid in the reform of the nation, and of the Church in particular, and, as its ultimate result, to spread scriptural holiness over the land.

From all this it will be seen that Wesley had no desire that a separate sect should be formed, although he made provision for it. If a sect was already formed, it was through no fault of his; and if he made provision for the perpetuity of his work separate from the Church of England, it was by constraint, the constraint of those who had refused to make a home for it within the Church, a work that ought to have had a place there, but which was of too great importance to be destroyed if that place were denied it. Wesley had to choose between trying to keep Methodism in alliance with the Church, which he so much loved, without any provision for its continuance in case of his failure, and the making a provision for its permanency after he was taken away. He judged the continuance of Methodism, with all the attendant evils of another separate Christian community, to be a better thing in the interests of Christianity in the earth than its abolition would be; and I think all but the most bigoted will approve his decision. He therefore drafted his "Deed of Declaration," embracing the doctrinal basis of Wesleyan Methodism, and appointing a ruling Head in a Conference of one hundred preachers; and he ordained ministers. Having thus constituted Methodism a corporate society, he anticipated, as he said when laying the foundation-stone of the City Road Chapel, that it would remain "till the earth and the works thereof are burnt up."

To these evangelists, these builders of Methodism, no idea presented itself of founding a separate denomination. They did not desire it; they strove to prevent it. If the developed Methodism of to-day is a separate Church, the fault (if it be one) lies outside the denomination itself. We will not be charged with the responsibility of the separation of Methodism from the Church of England. All English Methodism to-day might have been included within the Church if they, who from within repudiated and spurned it and cast it out, had been animated by the right spirit, and had hailed these men as heaven-sent messengers, and their work as a heaven-wrought work. But no, alas! that spirit did not exist. It was to this early and long-continued repudiation that the coldness towards the Church observable amongst the Methodists was due. The seeds of this repellent spirit brought forth fruit after their own kind.

Wesley went down to his grave disappointed that the great work had not been recognised and promoted by the Church and sheltered within its bounds.[1] It is often said

[1] See Appendix C.

to-day, especially by certain of the clergy, that Wesley did not wish his people to leave the Church. Most certainly he did not; and the blame of their leaving was at the door of the men of that day who would not, or could not, see the real greatness of the work, and its harmony, as a work of God, with the true work of the Church.

2. *Further Historical Development.*

(1) *Its Effective Vindication of the Truth.*

When Wesley and his band of coadjutors arose and went into the fields, they gathered around them a motley mass of untrained, unthinking, unreasoning, irreligious men, women, and youths, from whom they encountered rudeness and external violence. But when their teaching came before the writers and thinkers, the men of letters, or the public instructors of the age, they encountered other conditions. There were views widely diffused and earnestly defended in the Churches which the Methodist band judged, and rightly judged, to be opposed to the teachings of Holy Scripture; some of them were dangerous enough, and destructive of Christian life and principles. It is right to notice that Wesley and his companions wrought in strict accordance with what they judged to be the spirit, and the discipline, and certainly with the true doctrine of the Church of England.

Wesley himself was a disputant of no mean order, but his contentions were not as Luther's, against the teachings of the Church, but for them. He was one of the most efficient defenders of the faith of the Church of England in the century. His was not a reformation of Church doctrine, but of men's morals. He made no pretensions to the discovery of new principles or new truths. He had no new doctrines and no new features of religious life and conduct. It was his constant boast that all his truths were old truths, and all his doctrines the doctrines taught by the fathers of the Church at the beginning, of which every detail may be traced to apostolic types.[1]

While always careful to support his views by an appeal to the authoritative writings of the Church of England, he never satisfied himself without a final appeal to the fountain of all that authority—the Holy Scriptures. Methodism was a movement born within the Church of England, and, to the honour of that Church, it was born of it; and it grew up in harmony with the best traditions of the Church. The Methodist reformation was carried on by means of the Church's doctrines; but it was a revivifying of them; and, by the infusion of a more vigorous life, it expanded them as the bud is expanded by the warm breath of spring before the early summer's sun.

Wesley's theology, in its attitude towards the general religious belief of the Churches of this country in the last century, as a protest against deadly errors, and as a defence of the time-honoured teachings of the Church of England, was of the highest importance. Grave errors in doctrine were rife, some of them were spread widely abroad; and as the upspringing of a free, vigorous, earnest religious life, Methodism was destined to come into conflict with them. Indeed, it seems to have been a part

---

[1] This subject is treated at length and with great ability in a previous lecture—*Methodism in the Light of the Early Church* (Fernley Lecture for 1885), by William F. Slater, M.A.

of its calling to raise its voice of antagonism against them.

Wesley had not completed the first year of what he regarded as his new life ere he came into collision with forms of religious belief and practice from which he felt himself compelled to dissent. He found the first symptom of defection amongst his friends the Moravians, to whom he owed so much, and for whom he had so sincere an admiration. The first dawn of error, the combating of which formed so important a part of his work, and occupied so much of his time and thought, was in the mystic doctrine of "stillness," into which, in their simplicity, they were unconsciously and too easily led by specious and deceitful teaching.

The little Society at Fetter Lane, where Wesley often expounded, and where he had learned to love and admire the Moravians, with whom he was joined in intimate fellowship, became, through the influence of one or two false teachers, deeply infected with the strange mystic error that until men had faith they should not use the means of grace. It is almost impossible for us to imagine that a Church professing to be Christian, and so highly to be honoured as the Moravian Church deserved to be, could ever have been tainted with views so grossly at variance from Christian teaching as the following:—"The way to attain faith in Christ is to wait for Christ, and be still— *i.e.* not to use the means of grace, not to go to church, not to communicate, not to fast, not to use so much as private prayer, not to read the Scriptures;"—these being held not to be means of grace to unbelievers. They were also taught that they should neither do temporal good nor

The Mission of Methodism Defined. 97

attempt to do spiritual good, and that those who were not clean should not use the means, and those who were need not.

Sad was the condition of the Fetter Lane Society. With great and patient effort Wesley strove, in private and public, with pen and with voice, to eradicate this error; but in vain. And at length, as we have seen, he felt he could no longer continue in fellowship with a people so seriously tainted with injurious error.

But Wesley is soon pressed with another form of error, the mention of which brings pain to our hearts. I refer to those views which are so generally comprehended under the word "Calvinism"—the doctrines of unconditional election and reprobation, of the limited extent of the atonement, and others relating to the perseverance of saints and kindred subjects. The effects of Wesley's work in combating these errors is seen to-day in a field too wide to be hastily viewed. He preached and taught and wrote against them. He raised up a band of men of his own views, and sent them through the country proclaiming salvation to all men. He met the Calvinistic error by his public offer of salvation to every sinner, and by laying the blame of non-salvation at the door of every one who refused to yield to the strivings of the Divine Spirit.

That there is a Calvinistic interpretation of the Articles of Religion is well known. Wesley stood forward with his doctrine of a free salvation open to all on repentance and abandonment of evil. He was in this sense a true Arminian, but he was as clear as Calvin himself in his avowal of the absolute dependence of the sinner on the grace of the Holy Spirit, as taught by the best of the Church of England and the Puritan divines. To them Wesley was faithful; to them Methodism has hitherto been faithful.

It was here that Wesley came into collision with his bosom friend, Whitefield, with John Cennick, and others. On this subject he preached in this city his sermon on "Free Grace," which was the immediate cause of the rupture between himself and Whitefield; but private friendships must be sacrificed, as everything else was sacrificed, to the claims of truth, conviction, and right. The sermon was followed by other publications in opposition to Calvinism —" Serious Considerations concerning the Doctrines of Election and Reprobation," an extract from Dr. Watts; also an extract from the writings of Richard Baxter, entitled " Some Considerations on Absolute Predestination ; " afterwards by another extract on " The Scripture Doctrine concerning Predestination, Election, and Reprobation ; " also " A Dialogue between a Predestinarian and his Friend ; " " A Dialogue between an Antinomian and his Friend ; " a second " Dialogue ; " and subsequently similar writings on " The Perseverance of the Saints " and " Predestination."

At the same time another voice was heard. With the free flow of mellifluous verse Charles Wesley sang out the universal love of God, His all-redeeming grace; and the amplest doctrines of free grace were proclaimed in those heart-stirring hymns which from that time to this have re-echoed in the vales and villages as well as in the towns of our own country and over many a wide plain in far-off lands.

If Wesley's controversial writings were not large, they were trenchant. They were intended for the people, and were fitted to help them to just scriptural views. One reason why he does not appear as a theological writer is that he accepted a complete system of theology, and he had no practical purpose to serve by extensive writing on abstruse questions. But it was less by printed books than by the living voice that he both published and defended the free, gracious call of the gospel and the purity and obligation of the divine law. It was the clear and wide proclamation of the truth that drove the error from the field, as the morning beams chase the gloom of night.

Another form of error which presented itself was Antinomianism. In Wesley this met with an uncompromising foe. Whatever may be thought by any concerning Wesley's theological teaching, none can accuse him of a want of loyalty to the holy law of God. He knew no godliness that was not practical godliness. He tells us, when speaking of the rise of Methodism so-called: "In 1729 my brother and I read the Bible; saw inward and outward holiness therein; followed after it, and incited others so to do. In 1737 we saw, 'This holiness comes by faith.' In 1738 we saw, 'We must be justified before we are sanctified.' But still holiness was our one point—inward and outward holiness. God then thrust us out, utterly against our will, to raise up a holy people. When Satan could not otherwise prevent this, he threw Calvinism in our way; and then Antinomianism, which struck at the root both of inward and outward holiness."[1] It must be obvious that here the emphasis is to be placed on the word "holiness." That was the question of questions with these men.

Thus, whilst it was characteristic of this great revival of religion that it declared the universality of the atoning sacrifice, the loving welcome awaiting every returning

[1] *Min. Conference*, 1765.

sinner, and the privilege of each believer to know his sins forgiven, the danger of this wide and free proclamation of mercy was not unobserved or unprovided for. Wesley knew, and his adherents have always known, as indeed it has been known ever since it was first proclaimed, that the doctrine of justification by faith is not to be taught without the complementary doctrine of good works. And no one can deny that this revival of religion was a revival of morality. The divine law was not lost in the splendour and amplitude of the divine love. Mercy and truth met together; righteousness and peace kissed each other. Embedded in the definite teachings of Methodism is a series of discourses on "The Sermon on the Mount." These models of the faithful enforcement of the practical duties of Christianity form part of the authoritative doctrinal standards of the Methodist Church to-day.

In the first Conference the question was asked, "What sins are consistent with justifying faith?" and the answer was as definite as the question was direct, "No wilful sin. If a believer sins wilfully, he casts away his faith." And, again, it was demanded, "Are works necessary to the continuance of faith?" Equally precise was the reply, "Without doubt; for a man may forfeit the free gift of God, either by sins of omission or commission." Seeing the danger, the members of the Conference exposed it, and placed strong barriers of truth against it. Thus Behmenish stillness, Calvinistic restriction, and Antinomian latitudinarianism, with its low views of Christian faith and lower views of the Christian life, met with fearless antagonists in the founders of Methodism. It must not escape notice how effectually Wesley secured for the bulk of the English people a freedom from these several errors. He did not stamp them out; but by his great evangelistic labour he permeated the active religious sentiment of the country with his own wide views of the redeeming work of our blessed Lord, and taught all men their interest in that redemption. Throughout the length and breadth of the land, in town and village, from highway and market cross, and over the face of green fields, the proclamation of a free, a full, a present salvation was made. Not only by the clearness of its teaching, and by the exhibition of the contradictions, the inconsistencies, and the unscripturalness of opposing theories, but by the rhythm of holy song and psalm was the great truth wafted on evening breeze and early morning air—

> "For all my Lord was crucified;
> For all, for all my Saviour died."

In attempting to spread scriptural holiness through the land, the exposure of doctrinal errors became inevitable. The indebtedness of the Churches of this country to the doctrinal purity of early and later Methodism is very great. If, with a religious upheaving such as was begun in 1739, and which so greatly engaged the sympathies and so deeply affected the lives of widespread multitudes, a leaven of error had been propagated, it is not easy to imagine how grievous the effect would have been.

Wesley must certainly appear as the champion of the purity and integrity of Christian doctrine of the eighteenth century. His influence in combating error has not always been duly appreciated. What stood in the face of the extravagances of Mysticism and Socinianism, of the dangers of Calvinism and of Antinomian irreligion at that day, as Methodism did? Wesley had no new truth; he professed to have none. He was not raised up to proclaim one. He had no mission to declare one. But he found old truths rusty and hidden beneath encrusting errors—forgotten, out of mind—and he set them forth in their brightness before the eyes of the world; and it is the mission of his followers ever to keep them bright. In saying that Methodism, whether represented by Wesley in the past, or by its writers and teachers in the present, is true to the doctrine of the Church of England, it is needful to keep in mind what that doctrine really is. If the High Church interpretation be the true one, then Wesley did depart, and Methodism has ever departed, and one of its recognised obligations is still to depart from it, and that not silently, but by the tones of a clear, distinct, and emphatic teaching. It is, however, fair to Wesley to say that he sincerely believed himself to be an exponent of the true doctrine of his Church.

Methodism bore then, and it has ever since borne, its clear testimony to the general sinfulness of the race;[1] to the universal need of redemption, and to its universal provision; to the inclusion of every son of Adam in the gracious purposes of the gospel; to the inability of men to do any good thing without the grace of the Holy Spirit, and to the great principle that, forasmuch as "a measure of the Spirit is given to every man to profit withal," every disobedient one stands condemned. In its teachings every one is included in the permission to know himself saved of the Lord, by a clear inward conviction, not wrought by

---

[1] I must here refer to Wesley's reply to Dr. Taylor, of Norwich, contained in his treatise on "Original Sin," a work which is a model of controversy, and shows Wesley's power as a theological writer.

authority of human voice, whencesoever that authority is derived, nor by the sole pledge of sacramental or other services, but by the faith of the operation of God. It declares the equal permission of all to share in a freedom from the condemnation and the power of sin, in the happiness of a joyful salvation, in the attainment of settled peace, of holy joy, of comfortable hope, and of a faith that triumphs over the world and self. It declares all may do the will of God in freedom, and the inflexible duty of all so to do, as well as to love the Lord God with all the heart, mind, soul, and strength, and the neighbour equally with the self.

(2) *Influence on Church and Dissent, and on National Manners and Morals.*

In tracing the further historical development of the mission of Methodism, it is needful to speak of the revival of the religious spirit in Church and Dissent by its instrumentality. Wesley, at an early period, judged that a part of the divine purpose, in calling Methodism into existence, was to purify the Church, as well as generally to spread principles of true religion broadcast over the land. That such was its effect has been most candidly acknowledged and amply illustrated on all hands, and does not now require demonstration. Its influence reached to all the Churches. To it may be traced the quickening, if not the re-creation of the Evangelical party in the Church of England. It gave the first impulse to the religious fervour which issued in the Tractarian movement. To the Dissenting Churches it was the breath of fresh life—" the bracing breeze which had come sweeping down from the hills of Methodism over Baptist meadows, as well as Independent fields."[1] The Society of Friends shared in the spiritual benefit it was the honoured instrument of diffusing. And all the existing Christian activities received a new impulse, and many new ones of great value were called into existence by it directly or indirectly. But its influence was not confined to the Societies that were gathered, or to the existing Churches; it extended to the masses of the people who were outside, and whose deplorable state was the call for its interposition. In the words of Mr. Leslie Stephen, Wesley "forced more serious thought upon the age."

I am most wishful, in trying to estimate the influence of Methodism on the Christian life of this country, to guard against viewing it with the pardonable prejudice which an attached son, whose filial regard for its great leaders is very profound, might easily be led to indulge. I acknowledge that it is almost an impertinence to the good sense and general intelligence of this hour to summon testimonies to the beneficent character of that work, at the head of which stand the honoured names so often quoted in the preceding pages.

Happily, this subject has been treated at considerable length, and from various points of view, by many competent and independent writers, and after the progress of events has given ample opportunity for forming a just judgment. And I refer with pleasure to the testimonies of a wide range of writers who have judged Methodism from without, and estimated its work alongside that of other Christian communities. That work has formed the subject of philo-

[1] Stoughton.

sophical disquisition and of severe critical analysis, as well as of dispassionate history. Not only have the best writers in the English and American Methodist Churches, who might be thought to be naturally somewhat prejudiced in their judgment, pronounced upon it, but it has been regarded from the points of view occupied by the several parties in the Church of England, by the Dissenters, and by others who represent the literary rather than the religious judgment, the result being a wealth and variety of testimony to its beneficent influence from men who could be biassed by no party prejudice, whose disinterested judgments it is at once a pleasure and an instruction to collate.

It is not necessary that I should reproduce the descriptions given of the state of English society, or of the condition of the Churches generally,[1] alike the Established and the Dissenting Churches,[2] in the early part of the last century. My time and other limits imposed upon me prevent me from tracing this with any minuteness, and there is the less need that I should attempt it, although it is germane to my subject, seeing it has been done with so much fulness and minuteness of detail by many writers. I shall illustrate this by a few references, all tending to show the bearing of Wesley's work on the Churches of the land, and on the general national manners. And though each writer may, from his own point of view, find occasion to dissent from some of Wesley's teachings or

---

[1] "For nearly a century the policy of stamping out enthusiasm was pursued, and the end was a state of unfaith, ungodliness, and unrighteousness, such as has no parallel in our history."—(Rogers, p. 125.)

[2] "Nor can it be said that the Establishment alone was responsible; there was much neglect on the part of the old Dissent."—(Stoughton, vol. vii. p. xvii.)

methods, yet all bear witness to the worthiness of his aim, the goodness of his life, the unselfishness of his devotion, and the widespread, far-reaching, and beneficent influence of his labours.[1]

Mr. Leslie Stephen, while not omitting to expose what he judged to be weaknesses and failings of Wesley, has given a very high testimony to his work and his character. Southey, who did not spare the lash, when it so pleased him, was compelled to affirm that he considered Wesley as "the most influential mind of the last century, the man who will have produced the greatest effects centuries, or perhaps millenniums, hence, if the present race of men should continue so long." The late Dean Stanley declared that "Wesley and Whitefield did together a work such as never had been done before." Mr. Rogers says: "These two men (Wesley and Whitefield) shook England to its centre, and were the pioneers of a movement which has been nothing short of a revolution;" and, again, "Of all the great men of the century, there is not one who left on it a deeper impression, or did in it a more abiding work, than the self-denying and untiring worker, in labours abundant, as in spirit he was pure and unselfish, who laid the foundations of Wesleyan Methodism. . . . Which of them all has left a monument so enduring, or which of them is there the subtraction of whose teaching and influence would have been so real a calamity as the loss of the power wielded by Wesley?"

It was not Wesley's statesmanship that effected this great work, though he was "one of the most remarkable statesmen ever found in the Christian ministry,"[2] and "the first of

[1] See Appendix D.   [2] Rogers.

theological statesmen," and though "his genius for government was not inferior to that of Richelieu."[1] It was what Mr. Rogers calls "that spiritual enthusiasm which inspired Wesley and Whitefield," and which wrought the "marvellous revolution in the religious life of the country." Mr. Leslie Stephen affirms that "Wesleyanism is, in many respects, by far the most important phenomenon of the century;"[2] and in his philosophical estimate of it as one of the spiritual factors of the great revival, while criticising it with some severity, he very clearly traces its influence and power in the great religious reaction which that century witnessed. Canon Overton, whose knowledge of Methodism is most thorough, in his very candid review, forms the same generous estimate.[3] Mr. Guinness Rogers has written with equal appreciativeness and much warmth of admiration.[4] But, amongst the many writers on this subject, perhaps, for effectiveness, for interesting detail, for fairness and moderation, for breadth of view, combined with minuteness of treatment, Dr. Stoughton is pre-eminent.[5] He says, "The rise and progress of Methodism may be regarded as the most important ecclesiastical fact of modern times, and requires to be studied in relation to the Established Church of England, the old Nonconformist bodies, and the missionary interests of Christianity throughout the world by every one who would understand the

[1] Macaulay.
[2] *History of English Thought in Eighteenth Century*, vol. ii. p. 389.
[3] *The Evangelical Revival in the Eighteenth Century*, by John Henry Overton. See also *The English Church in the Eighteenth Century*, by Charles A. Abbey and John H. Overton.
[4] *The Church Systems in the Nineteenth Century:* The Sixth Congregational Lecture. By the Rev. J. Guinness Rogers, B.A.
[5] *History of Religion in England*, vol. vi. chaps. v. xi. xii. xvii.

religious history of the last hundred years." He has also traced the influence of the entire evangelical revival, not only on the existing Churches of the land, but on the general moral condition of the country, and on some of the world-wide philanthropic institutions, which do honour to our age.[1] Lecky judges that the splendid victories by land and sea, that formed the most dazzling episodes in the reign of George II., "must yield in real importance to that religious revolution which shortly before had been begun in England by the preaching of the Wesleys and of Whitefield."[2]

That Wesley's work was directly effective in producing a great revolution in the Church of England has been most abundantly acknowledged. And, perhaps, this change is one of the greatest benefits he conferred on the inhabitants of this country. The effect of his work on the different Evangelical Churches throughout the land was equally great; while its influence on Christian activities of all the Churches is discerned to this very day. To the revival of the last century was due that state of religious sensibility which led many good and true Churchmen in an earlier part of the present one to view with sorrow the dangers of a latitudinarian reaction in the Church of England, and which really stirred the spirits of the men who were instrumental in effecting the great change which we have witnessed rapidly progressing within the Church of England during the last fifty years—a change within the Church which

---

[1] "The work of Foreign Missions received an immense stimulus from the evangelical revival."—Overton.

[2] *A History of England in the Eighteenth Century*, by William Edward Hartpole Lecky.

takes its place beside that without the Church of the last century; and having, like it, so great issues for good, and concerning which I cannot cease to be devoutly and fervently thankful. It is another development of real religion, such as seems to have followed the great epochs of spiritual reawakening witnessed at successive periods of the Church's history,—another of the great tidal-waves of spiritual influence of which the Anglican Reformation of the sixteenth century, the Puritan of the seventeenth, and the Methodist of the eighteenth are special examples.

One historian, himself a member of the Oxford band of 1833, and a prime mover in the very first stages of that great spiritual revolution, has not withheld his testimony to the direct and beneficent, the " revivifying " power of the Methodist revival of the preceding century upon the Church of England, affirming it to have been " from this great movement that a reflex action passed over the whole Church." [1]

Undoubtedly the spirit of religious susceptibility which was manifest in the outburst of affirmed attachment to the Church's doctrine, ritual and discipline which immediately preceded the Tractarian movement, and was, indeed, the first public demonstration of the hidden power from which that movement issued, sprang originally from the great revival. I am not unmindful of the excesses in doctrine and ritual which, in our view, detract so much from the perfectness of that movement. But it is characteristic of great revulsions of thought that the recession from one extreme is often followed by a departure to the opposite one.

[1] *A Narrative of Events connected with the Publication of the Tracts for the Times.* By William Palmer.

Thus clear testimony is borne to Methodism as the chief power in promoting the revival, or, perhaps, I should say, the channel through which it pleased God to revive the Protestant Churches, not of this land only, but of others, both Continental and Transatlantic. The word revival is the true one. Methodism is essentially a revival, not a new creation. There is nothing new in it, save as a fresh development of that which is old may be called new. The doctrines are old; the Christian discipline is old; the spirit of labour is old; the philanthropy is old;—all is old. But as the breath of spring causes old roots to burst forth to new and more vigorous life, so the spirit which breathed through Methodism—an old spirit withal—caused that great revival of religion in this country, from which dates a new era in the spiritual history of mankind.[1]

Lecky describes the religion of England from the Revolution till the time when the Methodist movement had pervaded the Establishment with its spirit, as "cold, selfish, and unspiritual;" and he affirms: "The evangelical movement, which directly or indirectly originated with Wesley, produced a general revival of religious feeling, which has incalculably increased the efficiency of almost every religious body in the community." After referring to the revolutionary spirit in France, and its wide extension and perilous results, he says: "England on the whole escaped the contagion. Many causes conspired to save her, but

---

[1] "They (Wesley and Whitefield) breathed a new spirit into all the Churches; they wrought a great moral transformation in large classes of the people; they produced a perceptible change even on the society which branded them as wild fanatics."—(Rogers, p. 574.)

"An influence like the breath of spring came upon pulpit and press, upon home and public life."—(Stoughton, vol. vi. p. 390.)

among them a prominent place must, I believe, be given to the new and vehement religious enthusiasm which was at that very time passing through the middle and lower classes of the people."[1]

"No description could be more appropriate than that which designates the movement which delivered England from this condition as the Evangelical Revival. It was like new life from the dead to the Dissenting communities, to whom it came as a fresh inspiration; and it was new life to the multitudes who thrilled under the power of the evangelists who proclaimed the old truth with which they were so unfamiliar that it had to them the surprise of novelty and the force of a fresh revelation. By-and-by, also, it became a new life to the Established Church, which for long did its utmost to repress the enthusiasm and zeal which were destined to work in it a religion that has given it a new tenure of existence."[2]

What are these revivals of religion but the re-shining of "the Sun of Righteousness" upon His own still darkened world? Each is a fresh fulfilment of the great truth, "I will pour out My Spirit upon all flesh;" and each an additional pledge of its final fulfilment to the utmost millennial limit.

(3) *Foreign Missions.*

We have seen the mission of Methodism to have been keenly and sharply defined. Wesley, at least, knew to what he was called, although even his prescient eye did not discern the ultimate limits to which his work would extend, any more than he who first utilized the expansive

[1] Vol. ii. p. 634. [2] Rogers, p. 125.

power of steam knew to what his discovery would lead. It need hardly excite surprise that no reference is made to Foreign Missions in Wesley's definition of the purpose for which Methodism was raised up ; nor is prominence given to them as forming part of the calling of Methodism in the early Minutes. But Methodism has its mission to the nations nevertheless.

By these remarks I have no intention of suggesting that Wesley was indifferent to the condition of foreign nations, or to any efforts that might be suggested to alleviate that condition ; but solely that he did not at that time hold it to be a part of the calling and obligation of Methodism to undertake missions to the heathen. The Georgian missionary, who was so anxious to preach to the Indians, and so painfully disappointed when he was prevented from doing so, and who declared himself ready to go to Abyssinia or China, or whithersoever it should please God to call him to go on the holy errand, could not be indifferent to the claims of the heathen. He saw and keenly felt the deep necessities of his own country, and he was thoroughly convinced of the suitability of his means to meet those necessities in a very large degree. His words, however, are far from indicating that in his view Methodism could reach the entire need even of this nation, and he was too practical to spend time or thought on mere speculations in regard to other lands. But if he did not recognise any claim on his Societies to undertake missions to the heathen, he could not have better prepared the way for such missions, or have done a greater service to the world, than by rendering the service to his own country he was permitted and honoured to render.

Although Wesley does not in so many words declare

the purpose of God in raising up the Methodists to be to spread the gospel to the ends of the earth, yet, doubtless, was it one of the hidden purposes of the Divine Providence which revealed themselves one by one as Methodism was able to fulfil them. Subsequent history must be appealed to to show how far it was fitted to do this greater work. In its adaptations must its calling and mission be indicated.

Wesley could hardly be expected to cope with this additional work. There was a limit even to his energy and activity. He had enough to do at home. Besides which, he was pressed between financial difficulties and the growing demands of the work in this country, demands that he could not hope fully to overtake. Moreover, the new Churches were not yet prepared: Methodism could spare neither men nor money. But in due time it pleased God to prepare the way. A coadjutor was raised up in the person of Dr. Coke, who, with his personal endowments, his profound interest in missions, and his ability to help both by his own private fortune and by his fervent appeals for pecuniary aid from others, was enabled to initiate a work which has been the glory and crown of Methodism from that hour to this. In the provision of such a helper at the critical moment we must recognise another of the many signal interpositions of Providence by which this whole movement has been distinguished.

It is not to be forgotten that no modern, perhaps no earlier ministers, ever held so firmly to the great truth of the adaptation of the gospel to all men, of its provision for all, or of its final extension to all, as did the Methodist preachers.

Never did any Church *sing* this great truth as the Methodists have sung it, although in the earliest hymn-books we do not catch so definitely as afterwards the strains of universal redemption or the earnest cry for the extension of the gospel to all. There was that close concentration of thought upon the spiritual interests of the individual soul that characterized John's words for some weeks after his own conversion, and which was natural enough after the prolonged struggle through which the new psalmists had so recently passed. But very soon wider sympathies burst forth, and we hear Charles Wesley, and with him the young Methodist Societies, singing out with gladness the "everlasting love to man." He called upon all to share with him the life divine. He proclaimed the gates of the kingdom of heaven open for all returning sinners. There was no exclusiveness in creed, or minstrel liturgy, or teaching heard in the first preaching-houses or the open fields. The very first hymn of our book is indicative of the spirit of the whole—

> "O for a thousand tongues, to sing
> My great Redeemer's praise!"
> . . . . . .
> "Look unto Him, ye nations; own
> Your God, ye fallen race."

And the second is like—

> "Come, sinners, to the gospel feast,
> Let every soul be Jesu's guest."

And the fourth follows in the same strain—

> "Ho! every one that thirsts, draw nigh;
> 'Tis God invites the fallen race."

Nor can I forget the thirty-fourth—the most perfect of the series—

> "O for a trumpet voice
> On all the world to call!
> To bid their hearts rejoice
> In Him Who died for all;
> For all my Lord was crucified;
> For all, for all my Saviour died."

But it must be said that it was probably the universality of the gospel message, in opposition to the Calvinistic restriction, more than the thought of the actual spread of the gospel amongst the nations, that drew forth these precious strains.

That these hymns fostered in Methodism the spirit of deep pitifulness for all mankind, and helped to train its sons into a profound sympathy with

> "The heathen lands that lie beneath
> The shades of overspreading death,"

many of us know and have long felt. The belief in the universal redemption must precede the hope of the universal recovery. The *Arminian Magazine* prepares the way for the Missionary Report. That the Calvinistic theory must have arrested the Church's effort is all too obvious.

There was no more suitable soil into which the seeds of missionary zeal could be cast than was afforded by the people who, raised from a semi-heathen darkness or a spiritual lethargy, had been quickened truly to apprehend the supreme dignity of life, the degradation and danger of evil, and the gladness of a joyful salvation, and who had been fired with love to man by the manifested love of God to themselves.

The inception of Foreign Missions as a part of the work of Methodism is in the very terse words of certain questions proposed in the Conference of 1769. *Question* xii. runs thus, "What is reserved for contingent expenses?"—*Answer.* "Nothing." *Question* xiii. "We have a pressing call from our brethren at New York (who have built a preaching-house), to come over and help them. Who is willing to go?"—*Answer.* "Richard Boardman and Joseph Pilmoor." *Question* xiv. "What can we do further in token of our brotherly love?"—*Answer.* "Let us now make a collection among ourselves." *Question* xv. "What is the whole debt remaining?"—*Answer.* "Between five and six thousand pounds."

So between the pressure of two financial difficulties, a heavy debt on the one hand, and nothing reserved for contingencies on the other, they make their collection; and the great American Mission starts in the English Methodist Conference. In the following year the "stations" contain this entry:—"America: Joseph Pilmoor, Richard Boardman, Robert Williams, John King." The work in America is begun.

Again, we find in the next year (1771) these words occur:—"*Question* vii. Our brethren in America call loudly for help. Who are willing to go over and help them?" Five were willing; two—Francis Asbury and Richard Wright—were sent. No one then could foresee that one of those two, a young man of six-and-twenty summers, tall in person, grave in demeanour, was destined to become an apostle whose labours would equal those of any servant of the Cross whose name is inscribed on the rolls of the Church since the apostolic age. Two years afterwards eight names appear. In five years from that date (1778), there are 6968 members recorded. In 1784, Thomas Coke, who had been associated with Wesley in London for six years, was appointed to America; and in course of the year he and Asbury were ordained superintendents, a term which the American brethren soon changed to bishops.[1]

This ordination by Wesley was in every respect a most important step. It made provision for the spiritual service of the American Churches, which now were left by their own pastors; it introduced to that country a form of Church government which, judged by subsequent years, is proved to have been most singularly adapted to the necessities of the country, and it prepared the way for the constitution of Methodism as a separate and complete Church, and for the important changes in the relation of the Methodist Societies of this country to the Established Church of England.

In that same year Wesley attempted to deal with the wider question of missions to the heathen. He says: "I desired all our preachers to meet and consider thoroughly the proposal of sending missionaries to the East Indies. After the matter had been fully considered, we were unanimous in our judgment that we have no call thither YET, no invitation, no providential opening of any kind."[2] Like the apostles, he waited for the cry, "Come over and help us." This was in 1784. It is singular that the extract I have just read is the only reference to missions indexed in his collected works.

I do not forget his sermon on "The General Spread of

---

[1] Cf. *Bishop Asbury: a Biographical Study.* By Rev. F. W. Briggs.
[2] *Works*, vol. iv. p. 266.

the Gospel," published in the following year, in which he so darkly pictures the condition of the world, and in which he anticipates the spread of the gospel throughout all lands; and there is the quiet persuasion that the work of God, which had been witnessed in this country and in America, was only the beginning of a far greater work,—the dawn of "the latter-day glory;" a work which he believed would silently increase and spread "from heart to heart, from house to house, from town to town, from one kingdom to another." Beautiful indeed is the picture which he draws of the final spread of the gospel, and the effect of its universal diffusion. But there is no suggestion that it weighed upon his mind as a pressing duty of the Methodists of that hour to make special effort to send the gospel to other lands.

There is another indication of the greatness and solemn character of the mission of Methodism afforded in its adaptation to the newly forming English colonies, and especially in its being raised up simultaneously with the commencement of the present colonizing era. It was written a short time ago,[1] "The world is passing into the hands of the English-speaking races. Already the English tongue is the *lingua franca* of the planet. Already the territories over which the laws are made and administered in the language of Shakespeare and of Bacon exceed in wealth, in extent, in the number of their populations, and in the limitless latent possibilities of their development, all other lands ruled by all the sovereigns of the earth. In a hundred years, unless the progress of this marvellous transformation is suddenly checked

[1] *Contemporary Review*, August, 1889, p. 17, Art. *Papacy.*

in some manner as yet inconceivable, the English speakers will outnumber all the men of other tongues in the world."

Was it not a noble mission to have been called and qualified to be the chosen instrument in the moral elevation and spiritual quickening of such a people? and must it not unquestionably appear to have been a part of a great purpose in the raising up of Methodism at this opportune moment, when the English-speaking populations were beginning to spread themselves rapidly over the earth? It had gained a strength and an influence in this country. It was sufficiently *formed* to preserve a definite character, and yet it was sufficiently plastic to adapt itself to the necessities of any new conditions, and especially to those of newly established communities.

That a system of religious teaching so expansive in its evangelical Arminianism, so fervent in its evangelistic labour, inspired with such generous sentiments and purposes, calling into play the best energies of the individual spirit, and recognising so clearly the individual responsibility, should have been raised up at this important juncture, was a most gracious coincidence, and carried with it all the appearance of a wise and beneficent design.

It is impossible to contemplate without trembling the probable consequences to the newly forming nations of the West, had their populations been allowed to congregate from all parts of the earth, and had no fervent spiritual Church agency been present to control the forming national character.

In the Address of the American Conference to the

English Conference, dated 1796, there was a prescient discernment of the great future that was before that nation, and of the best means to provide for it. They say, "We are humbly endeavouring to sow those seeds of grace which may grow up and spread in this immense country, which in ages to come will probably be the habitation of hundreds of millions."

What other system could have coped with the conditions of national life in America at the close of the last century when the English clergy left their flocks and returned home? How truly this was a "supplying the lack of service!" The descriptions of the state of national manners in America at the time are sad indeed.

It has long appeared to me that Methodism was prepared in England for the accomplishment of its greatest achievements in America and elsewhere, by its investiture of men and women of all positions with a measure of responsibility; its recognition of individual capability to serve; entrusting the responsibilities of offices of various kinds to men of any position, provided they had character, so that with the exodus of godly Cornish miners to Australia or South Africa, of English and Irish Methodist agriculturists to North and Western America and Canada, an occasion was given for the carrying of the gospel to newly rising nations. Each believer was endowed with a previously recognised power to "meet a class," to give an exhortation, to commence a Sunday school, or to preach. No territorial restriction stood in their way. They found men in sin, and sought to save them. Their zeal had been inflamed by scenes at home, and by a teaching concerning the value of souls and the freeness of the gospel. Their talents had been exercised, their best sympathies stirred, and their efforts could not but be fruitful. They needed no minister and no funds. In many instances the colonists themselves could pray and preach and gather their neighbours together for worship. They could build up "Societies" without neglecting their business. They but yielded to the strongest impulses of their hearts by doing so. There was no necessity to wait for organized Churches to send forth their emissaries. The cry of want was enough. Wherever a single believer was found, no other cry than that which came up from the untaught and ungodly near was needed; no authority was required but that which each felt himself to be obeying when he sought to save his perishing fellow-men. Thus the beautiful sight is presented to us of the members of this Society, happy in their holy toil, plodding on alike in the lanes of this land and on the highways of the nation's commerce.

Several features of Methodism contributed to this. Every true Methodist was brought to a happy assurance of reconciliation with God. Feeling within him both the throb of holy joy and the impulse of holy affection, he could not but desire the welfare of those around him. Then he had a definite idea of the needed change,—no one must be at rest until he find rest in Christ. From the hour of his Methodist birth he had been taught that it was his duty to try to help forward the salvation of his neighbour. In no religious community or system of religious activity was the cruel repudiation of fraternal responsibility, "Am I my brother's keeper?" more deeply and sharply condemned; and this same spirit must still be seen to be diffused through all the various organizations that have either broken loose from Methodism or have caught their first inspiration from it. This aptitude to follow and the actual following of the English-speaking populations is, in my judgment, one of the especial callings of the Divine Providence to this people. Wherever it went it was at home.

Methodism was further adapted for this colonial extension by its freedom from any centralization of power. Churches might be planted in different lands and take the complexion of those lands, adapting themselves to the national preferences. So long as they were weak they were supported or aided, but when able to guide their own affairs they were committed to the guidance of their own good sense and the gracious providence of God. The history of the Churches of America, Canada, Australia, South Africa, etc. etc., abundantly illustrates this.

There has been a great expansion of the Church of England in later days; but its very name is restrictive, and its action during the American rebellion left the field open for more enterprising and less restricted communities. Not only the Church of England but other of our English Churches have followed our colonies, and are now following them; yet they did so in the wake of the Methodists.

The history of Wesleyan Methodism declares more loudly than any mere arguments could do, ·that in the mission, for the fulfilment of which it was raised up, most assuredly Foreign Missions were included.

Wesley died in 1791. In the year immediately following a fresh field of missionary labour appears in view; 223 members are reported from Sierra Leone, around which place so many touching and tender memories have since

The Mission of Methodism Defined. 123

gathered. In 1785 missions had been begun in Nova Scotia, Newfoundland, and Antigua. There were fifty stations in America, and 21,000 members. In five years after (1790) the number of members is doubled. In 1890 that Church has "spread into bands." We are honoured to have with us at this Conference one of its bishops, whose Circuit, to use his own graphic words, "girdles the earth." Large Churches bearing the Methodist name, and conforming more or less nearly to the original type, but all having its essential characteristics, are found in the United States and in Canada; and from them missions have been established in South America, Japan, China, North and South India, in Africa, and many islands of the seas; besides the vast domestic missions with their thousands of missionaries. To these are to be added all the missions under the direction of the British Conference or of others affiliated to it; the whole forming an aggregate which places the entire Churches that come under the one designation, numerically at the head of all the Protestant Churches in the world. "*What hath God wrought!*"

CHAPTER III.

HOW FAR HAS METHODISM HITHERTO BEEN FAITHFUL TO THE ESSENTIAL IDEA OF ITS MISSION?

THE definition of the mission of Methodism which I have taken from the writings of Wesley is a clear and comprehensive setting forth of the divine calling, by him to whom it was addressed and by whom it was likely to be most accurately interpreted. It may be thought that there is in this delineation by Wesley's pen a spirit of presumption and unwarrantable self-confidence. Whether such a spirit lurks there or not, it must be confessed that there is great boldness indicated. Was Wesley justified in making this assertion? Had he reasonable ground for concluding that such a purpose was contemplated in the raising up of himself and his co-workers? Did there seem to be any probability that the irregular work in which he and they were engaged, and of which he was the leader, would be likely to exert an influence of so benign and extensive a character on the Church and on the nation at large? What signs were present to warrant such an assurance? It is not difficult to find an answer to these questions. It may be safely asserted that the work was not undertaken in vanity and self-assurance. Nor was the definition of the work attempted until it was evident to Wesley and those around him that the work to which they had been led (as they believed providentially) was likely to secure these ends.

Wesley saw to how great a degree the Church had sunk into a condition of which apathy was but a minor fault. He had direct intercourse with large numbers of persons in different parts of the country, and had been brought into contact with every phase of the Church life of the hour. His own spiritual perceptions had been quickened by the change which he had undergone. He had himself experienced the power of the gospel. He had daily, almost hourly, evidence of the wonderfully transforming effect of his own preaching and of that of his companions. It was not uncommon for him to witness how eagerly the people responded to their earnest and faithful pulpit ministrations. Churches were crowded. Thousands of persons gathered wherever the evangelists went. He saw also the effect upon the clergy; for though many derided him and despised his work, and treated his followers with so much contumely that when they would fain have become devoted Church people they were driven off by rudeness and hard speeches, yet others rejoiced in the work, and, strengthened by its progress, were themselves encouraged to imitations of the methods employed—" provoked to jealousy;" and some of no mean note even joined themselves to the sect, and rejoiced to be called Methodists. As a true son of the Church, Wesley judged that the great spiritual revolution must be accomplished by the agencies of the Church and within its boundaries, and that it must be by the Church sustained and carried forward.

The wonderful effects of the new preaching; the confidence inspired by the joyful freedom which he felt in proclaiming a free gospel to all men; the state of religious enthusiasm that was produced by the fervid publication of the good news, not by himself or by his brother or Whitefield only, but by the itinerant lay-preachers sent out by him; the evidences of a revived religious life such as had not its parallel in any period of the Church's history since the Reformation,[1] which he would feel himself warranted in concluding was a work of God; and the strong, irresistible constraint within him, which he could only regard as the call of the Divine Spirit;—these, together with other indications that were present, may well have justified his belief that "God was about to do a great work in the earth," and that he and his co-workers were raised up by Divine Providence to be the instruments in promoting that work.

To constitute ourselves judges of these things it seems almost necessary that we should not stand, where we are compelled to stand, on a lower level than they whose work we are trying to appraise.

It was indeed a bold assertion. Judging from the best descriptions of the condition of the Church and of the nation at large that are available, there was a loud and pressing call for a radical change. This I have not need to stay to prove. The testimonies that have been gathered from many sources justify the conclusion that the Church was seriously lacking in the degree to which her true doctrinal teachings were apprehended and maintained, in

---

[1] "By the 'foolishness of preaching' the heart of England was stirred to its very depths, and stirred as it had not been since the days of the Reformation. Indeed, it is extremely doubtful whether, at the period of the Reformation, the English people were as deeply and widely moved as they were by the preaching of Wesley and of Whitefield."—(Rogers, p. 127.)

the manner of life of a large number of the clergy, in the character of the Church services and of Christian activities. If we test the Church on any of the four elements which I have called the essential elements of Methodism, how sadly shall we find it to be wanting! Where were the evidences of a spiritual conversion? Its necessity was not taught, or, as a rule, believed in. What was the standard of the Christian life and character? How many grievous faults of conduct were held to be consistent with a Christian profession! To what degree was Christian fellowship—a true communion of saints—understood or enjoyed? The struggle of the small Societies established by Dr. Woodward and others indicates both the necessity for closer Christian communion and the slight extent to which it obtained. And what amount of evangelistic effort was being put forth?

On all these points the Church must be held to have been miserably defective and faulty, even if we take the less severe judgments passed upon it by them who, living at the time, were best able to judge. Here and there a solitary clergyman strove to stem the current of national immorality and spiritual indifference; but it was a work which could not be done by a few men confined within the limits of individual and even widely separated parishes. The revival of religion in the last century was mainly effected, and perhaps could have been effected only by travelling preachers.

It must be remembered that Wesley did not put his work and the work of his companions on the same level with the ordinary work of the parish clergy. They were raised up " to supply the lack of service " of the ordinary ministers—to fill up a gap. This was Wesley's lowly view of what has proved itself to be so great a work. How far is this removed from presumption! They were "extraordinary messengers—out of the ordinary way." This was necessary. If their influence must be widespread, they must not be confined to small areas. If the "parish" was not conterminous with the "world," it must at least reach to the limits of the kingdom. Now what probability was there that these men would be able in any great degree to effect this change?

Few persons in these days fail to recognise in Wesley an agent of Divine Providence for the accomplishment of a great work in the world; or doubt that he was qualified for such a work by his personal endowments, as he was to be the leader of a band of men, who, by their almost superhuman labours, were able to accomplish so much. We see in him a true son of the Church, a very Hebrew of the Hebrews, a cultured clergyman, a Fellow and tutor of his college, an accomplished preacher, a man of extraordinary activity, a labourer who put all others to the blush, an ascetic, an embodiment of self-denying charity, of great precision, alike in mental process and in the habits of his life, and having a power of organization which has excited the astonishment of every student of his wonderful career. Then he had by his qualifications access to the pulpits of the land, if he became debarred from them by his excessive zeal. He spoke from within the Church. He was not an alien, but a son—a devoted, an admiring, a loving son. He broached no new doctrine. He had no antagonism to wage against the Church: he was ready to lay down his life in her service. He aimed not to destroy or undermine her true and rightful influence over the people. He set up no rival sect. He not only clung himself to the venerable establishment, but he bound his people to it; literally compelling them to go to church,[1] even though many of them had not been accustomed to do so before. "If you will not go to church," said he, "I will not come to you."

All these circumstances contributed to make him a most highly fitted instrument to effect a work both within and without the Church; even his exclusion from her pulpits brought him into contact with multitudes upon multitudes whose ear he could not have gained had he continued to occupy them. His great companions, Charles Wesley, Whitefield, and Fletcher, were also eminent clergymen, each in his own measure possessing the highest qualifications for usefulness, and standing abreast with their great leader. In addition to these, other clergymen stood by him from the first, even worked with him; while others were encouraged and stimulated by the contagion of his example. Besides which, he had the support of the essential teachings of the Church. The liturgy, the homilies, the great writers of the Church were in league with him. He preached the Church's doctrine; he honoured the Church's discipline; he seized upon the Church's true idea; he taught nothing that he could not support by the highest Church authorities. To spread scriptural holiness throughout the land was only carrying out the true design of the Church's existence. So that the momentum of the Church's true movement was with him. However contrary winds might blow, the set of the tide was in his favour.

[1] Except in a few cases, *e.g.* where the clergyman was an Arian.

But the Methodists probably wrought more effectually upon the Church by their influence upon the people, whence the ranks of true and faithful Churchmen were recruited. The force of a growing public opinion in favour of goodness would tend to correct abuses in the Church, and to arouse her ministers from their apathy.

As to the methods employed by Wesley. If he did not beforehand judge them to be the most suitable, they proved themselves to be so; and his work was rather the prudent use of means which the necessities of the moment called for or suggested, than of such as by predetermination were adopted. He was ready to avail himself of any expedient by which his one object could be gained. His mind was open (some persons think too open) to suggestions from any source. His system was elastic; he was bound by no rigid theories. Whatever principles guided him were purely of a practical, not a theoretical character. Nothing, for example, could have been more suitable as a chief method than the field-preaching—bringing him into contact with the multitudes who never darkened the church doors. It was a literal seeking of lost sheep in order to save.

The traversing and re-traversing the whole area of the country year by year for so long a time gave a unity and continuity to his work which it could not have acquired by a few and occasional and uncertain visits. He thus brought the great question of personal religion before the mind of the nation, and he kept it before it for half a century together, and with a force of persuasion which compelled men to see their interest in it.

In our time the daily press awakens the public mind to grave questions, and keeps them before the public attention;

but in those days, when no such powerful instrument was available, the living voice had to supply the lack. And the interesting spectacle rises before us of a cultured clergyman of impressive appearance and persuasive speech going through the land from one end to the other, undeterred by weather, by distance, by the difficulties of travel, or the thought of personal weariness; and without fear or presumption, but with kindly and gentle looks and pleasant voice, calling a half-awakened, ignorant, half-besotted people to contemplate great truths made plain and comforting, healing truths brought home to their comprehension; and all done in a spirit of self-sacrifice which added a charm to his message, and was an inspiration to himself.

Then the very truths that he taught, and the way in which they were taught, were other elements of fitness to the necessities of the hour. Many of his hearers were sunken in evil to so great a degree, and were so keenly proving its miserable and unsatisfactory condition, that there was little danger of its clear delineation failing to bring home conviction; while the unfolding of the divine gospel, and the gradually increasing numbers of living testimonies to its power and reality, could not but win the sick and sorrowful and faint to an eager attention, if not even to a glad acceptance, of its offer. After the first rude oppositions of the sinful, who were disturbed in their sinfulness, had passed away, the dissatisfaction with conditions so low created a craving for something higher and better; and the hungering and thirsting after righteousness was allayed by a satisfaction which as much astonished beholders as it gladdened its possessors.

Lecky has affirmed that the secret of the success of

Methodism was merely that it satisfied some of the strongest and most enduring wants of our nature, which found no gratification in the popular theology of the time, and that it revived a large class of religious doctrines which had been long almost neglected.[1]

Wesley wisely followed the example of the great apostles, who, when men and women had turned to the Lord as the result of their preaching and teaching, put the little band of believers under the guardianship of the most suitable persons they could find, committing them to this fostering care, and, leaving them, pursued their missionary path until the time should come when they could determine, "Let us go again and visit our brethren in every city where we have preached the word of the Lord, and see how they do" (Acts xv. 36). Then the method of gathering together the converts into classes and societies, the folding of the recovered sheep within an effectual protection, was another of the wise devices by which his work was both extended and preserved.

But we must lay an especial emphasis on that which he was the first to recognise and thankfully to acknowledge—the gracious divine help and blessing upon his labour. The gospel is not the power of man, but of God, to the saving of them that believe. There is a baptism of the Spirit, which alone can bring men to a new life. This Wesley knew; on this he relied, as his ministry, and that of all his helpers, whom he represents, abundantly testifies. We may conclude, with Mr. Rogers, that "the aspect of the country and the character of the people are the best testimony to the effects of Wesley's mission."[2]

[1] Vol. ii. p. 545.   [2] P. 575.

In presuming to inquire whether these men were faithful to this so great a calling, we are instantly met by the conviction that the greatness of that calling is to be estimated only by the greatness of their labour. They themselves alone discerned the real nature of their mission. They alone could see with what great work God had charged them. They alone felt its burden; they only could apprehend their responsibility. The work that they did exceeded their own designs. They were faithful above what observers could call faithfulness. Had their labour been diminished by one half, the world must still have held them to be faithful servants. Their indomitable zeal, their unselfishness, their utter disinterestedness and self-forgetfulness are to us an astonishment; and from that day to this present they have been for all evangelists typical examples of entire consecration, of holy devotion, of sacrificial labour, of intense fervour of spirit, of purity of motive, of heroic endurance, of successful and influential toil.

Fletcher was distinguished by an almost seraphic sanctity, but not less so for ceaseless, unwearied laboriousness of service, causing his name to be suggestive of the highest and best example of ministerial fidelity. Whitefield was not more remarkable for the overwhelming power of his oratory than for the free outpouring of his life in the most ungrudging service of his race. Charles Wesley, by his perpetual song, charms away the attention of observers from pulpit and pastoral labours, which alone were sufficient to make him worthy of a place amongst the most honoured of the clergy of his Church;[1] whilst John Wesley, a very

---

[1] "Charles Wesley was admitted to be one of the most eloquent, effective, and successful preachers of the age."—(Dr. B. Gregory, *Charles Wesley*.)

prince of preachers,[1] seems not to have been diverted for one moment throughout his long career from the plain path of imperative duty.

But it is not needful that I should eulogize the leaders in this great movement. They require no panegyric to-day. Their names stand as representatives of the best examples of godly devotion united with unstinted labour for the good of mankind. And if other names are not so familiar, it is not because their service was not great, but because it was impossible for ordinary examples, even of great usefulness, to escape eclipse in presence of these. It was no easy work for succeeding generations of Methodists to follow in the wake of such men, and to maintain such a work in any corresponding degree of efficiency.

But my immediate inquiry relates to the actual fulfilment of the mission entrusted to Methodism. Did Methodism, as a whole, answer with any degree of fidelity to the calling of God? It is quite possible for a few prominent leaders to redeem a community; and it is possible for men to dedicate themselves to great works without absolute fidelity to the essential demands of that work, and even without accomplishing that which they aimed to accomplish.

Wesley had his clerical coadjutors, chiefs who with fairly steady pace kept up with himself in holy toil, who stood in alliance with him in counsel, and were his peers in ability.

---

[1] Speaking of Wesley as a preacher, Dr. Stoughton says: "His preaching was very popular, much more so than is generally supposed. His fame in one respect has eclipsed his fame in another; but there is reason to believe if he had never organized the Methodist body he would have made an ineffaceable impression on the mind of England by his living voice. History, tradition, and a stream of invisible influences would have preserved his name as the most illustrious of preachers, next to one (Whitefield) already described." —(Vol. vi. p. 289.)

He had also his band of "helpers," who caught much of his spirit, and imitated his labour. And there were others who took their places as these one by one fell out of the ranks, worn down in early life by hard toil, or consumed by ardent zeal; and others again, who with steadier pace and calmer spirits did the work of evangelists to the multitudes, or of pastors to the gathered flocks. Nor must we omit the first missionaries, the pioneers of a noble band, the pæans of whose praise will one day be sung in many languages of the earth, when the fruits of their early labours shall be more evident, and those labours come to be estimated in presence of their ultimate results. Nor must we confine our thoughts to those who held sacred office. It is but simple justice to keep in view the faithful and attached followers, the combined brotherhood who together made up the totality of the United Methodist Societies.

Setting aside the question as to the fidelity of individuals, are we to judge that Methodism in its earlier periods was faithful to its calling? Was its true mission kept in view? Making due allowance for human frailty and imperfectness, did it to a reasonable degree effect that which it was raised up to effect? Was Wesley's limit of expectation reached? To what extent were the clergy stirred up to holy jealousy? Was the Church in any real degree revived and purified? Was the lack of service supplied? Was scriptural holiness spread over the land? Were the subsequent indications of Divine Providence in respect of the nations regarded and responded to? Was prominence given to the true doctrines of the gospel? Was the Church's ideal of the Christian life raised?—What shall be the answer to these questions? Would it be improper to say that, as far as the strength and zeal and honest toil of men could do these great things, they were done?

But other questions suggest themselves. Did Wesley suppose that the Methodists were raised up to continue their work until these ends were reached in the utmost degree? or did he intend by his words to affirm that they were raised up to set agoing a work which, in its manifold and ever-widening influence upon other agencies, would continue to operate unseen until ultimately these ends should be accomplished? It was certainly not in Wesley's expectation that within the compass of his own lifetime all these objects could be attained; and he evidently regarded Methodism as an abiding power, as, for example, when, in a sermon to which I have already alluded, he affirms his hope that the work begun in Oxford was "only the beginning of a far greater work—the dawn of the latter day glory;" and traces in imaginary lines the progress of the work from its small beginnings in his own day to its ultimate triumph in a millennium of blessing, when "universal holiness and happiness shall be established."[1]

We have already gained a true notion of that idea of the calling of Methodism which its founders and makers held before their eyes to guide them in the work for which, as they believed, God had raised them up, and to which they dedicated their efforts and their lives. We have also traced the development of this ideal—the formation of Methodism —to the death of Wesley. We cannot but conclude that to that time Methodism was true to itself; and the question now suggests itself, *How far have the successors to this first series*

[1] Sermon on "The General Spread of the Gospel."—(*Works*, vi. 282.)

of workers been faithful to the original calling? How far have they kept the same objects in view, and striven to accomplish the same ends? How far has Methodism up to this day been faithful to the idea of its mission? To speak of a work in which my own hands have taken a part, however small, is a very delicate task.

It is pleasing at the outset to quote the testimony of one who from careful observation was well fitted to judge. Dr. Stoughton says: "It is gratifying to add, on closing the record of Methodism in the eighteenth century, that the controversies raised after the death of Wesley do not seem to have interrupted the special work which he commenced."[1]

Wesley at his death left Methodism in its "quasi-alliance with the Church of England."[2] There was, however, amongst the Societies a strong undercurrent of dissent from it. Whether he was fully aware of this it is difficult to determine, though he was far from ignorant of it; and the sentence in his final revision of the Large Minutes, "not to found a new sect," seems to point to his fear of it. Be that as it may, he made provision for the continuance of his work, and evidently recognised the possibility of a total separation, though he deplored it; for he gave the example of an entirely distinct Church in the case of America; and he ordained some of his preachers, who were not clergymen of the Church of England, and who were not designed to labour in America, but amongst his own Societies both in Scotland and in England. This was separation indeed. Charles

---

[1] "Philosophical historians recognise, as all honest observers must recognise, the immense gain to the nation from the ministry of Wesley and Whitefield, and those who followed in their train."—(*Church System in the Nineteenth Century*, by J. Guinness Rogers, vol. vi. p. 293.)

[2] Dr. Rigg's *Church Organizations*.

Wesley, with Lord Mansfield, thought the American ordinations were.

Gradually the breach widened; gradually the Church party, as it was called, lost its strength, and ultimately (1795) a Plan of Pacification was formed, which, as its name indicates, was really a compromise. But may it not have been that a divine providence was leading to the formation of the separate community as a *necessity of the time?* The salvation of men was of more importance than the mere strengthening of a Church that lacked the life and power of godliness, as almost universal consent affirms to have been the case with the Church of England in the last century.

The period lying between Wesley's death in 1791 and the end of the century was one of much trial, strife, and danger. The leaders of the Connexion had the greatest difficulty in conducting it through this transition period. They struggled to adhere to its primitive character, but to adjust it to the new conditions; to contend with internal convulsions, and to overcome the loss of its honoured head and the diminution of its numbers.

Very soon after Wesley's death the Connexion was compelled to assume the position of a distinct and self-constituted Church, or it must have been dispersed altogether. This was seen in the struggles which began immediately after that event. But with unswerving fidelity the Conference from that day strove to proceed upon the lines laid down by Wesley. In fact, it was the strenuous adhesion to Wesley's principles that led to the first division in its ranks.

In the year 1797 a revision of the "Large Minutes" was

made by order of the Conference.[1] It is an interesting and equally important document. By this time Methodism had become less closely allied to the Church, and its adhesion was weakening. Strong forces were at work tending to separate them. There were two parties of differing sympathies both in the Conference and outside. Many of the ministers and some of the congregations clung to the Church, but many others had but little sympathy with it. Not a few of the people, ill-treated by their parish clergy, to whom they felt in no wise indebted for spiritual ministrations, were driven into an attitude of antagonism. Wesley himself could not during his lifetime wholly check this tendency. Notwithstanding all his influence, they formed a Methodism which was too strong for him.

As respected the Church, Methodism was now a receding tide. In the revised copy of the Minutes, "the Code of Regulations," the words "not to form a new sect" were struck out. It was indicative of the state of things. True, it was not desired by Wesley that "a new sect" should be formed; but, with what seemed to some a strange contradiction, he made provision for one. Methodism had indeed never formed any part of the Church organization;

[1] The following is the entry in an address "to the members and friends of the Methodist Societies:"—"Whereas we, the undersigned, have on this and the preceding day carefully revised the rules drawn up and left us by our late venerable father in the gospel, the Rev. Mr. Wesley, which were published by him in our Large Minutes, to which we consented when we were admitted, and by which we were regulated during his life; and whereas we have collected together those rules which we believe to be essential to the existence of Methodism, as well as others to which we have no objection; we do now voluntarily and in good faith sign our names as approving of and engaging to comply with the aforesaid collection of rules or code of laws, God being our helper."—(*Min. Conf.* 1797.)

it was never in any sense incorporated with the Church. It was an addition; and we know how Wesley strove to continue the members of his Society in attendance upon Church ordinances, the public services and the sacraments. But by his death the formation of the new Church was accelerated. For this he had made provision; and it was found that Methodism could subsist in entire independence of the Church. Why was a separate Church formed? Not because the leaders of Methodism desired it, for they strove hard to prevent it. But two causes operated to bring about this result. On the one hand, most of those who had been led into Wesley's Societies had not any real connection with the Church. The claiming them by the parochial clergy merely on the ground of their residence within the bounds of the parish was as effective as claiming the moon. They recorded no service received; they recognised no obligation; they said, "We never received religious instruction or help in the matter of our salvation." Many had to confess having received evil rather than good, suffering from the dislocating forces of rudeness and unkind treatment. How often did the clergy head the mob that assailed the little Methodist community! How often was the parson's voice the loudest and most frequently heard in the denunciation of the little Society, which might as well have been a Society within the Church (and if its founder's wishes had been attained would have been) rather than a Society which was driven out and driven off from it! If any blame rests upon any persons for the separate existence of Methodism, that blame lies mainly with a misguided clergy, who could not see, or would not, the work of God that was before their eyes, or cast their sheltering arms around sheep that sought the true fold. On the other hand, these people felt themselves indebted to the Methodists, who had brought salvation to their doors, and who had led them to repentance and righteousness; the work incumbent on the clergy, but by them unperformed. Was it any wonder that the strong hand of Wesley failed to keep his Societies in connection with the Church, as he desired, when both he and his people were ridiculed, opposed, despised? When that hand was stiffened by death, the effort was bravely made by many of the leaders of Methodism to carry out Wesley's wish. But what he had failed to do they were not likely to accomplish, when the strong bond of sympathy between the fretted people and the instrument of their salvation had been snapped by death.

One hundred years separate us from the death of Wesley, years of extraordinary national progress; an unequalled century in the history of the human race. How far has Methodism continued faithful during this period—a sufficient length of time in which to test its principles and methods of working, and its capability to adapt itself to varying conditions of national life? It cannot be denied, nor need it, that Methodism to-day differs in some respects from the Methodism of the last century; but these differences are in external form, not in any essential particular. In respect of the distinguishing characteristics of the system, as I have described them, I am bold to affirm that throughout the past century they have been faithfully adhered to, and that the Methodism of to-day is well related to its original idea.

We find the necessity for *conversion*, its possibility to all, and the joyous, free, exulting assurance of salvation through faith in Jesus Christ, have been held to the present hour. There is no abatement here. There is no occasion to mourn over any declension in doctrine on this first and most important subject. If individual men have not appeared to be gifted with powers which made many in the earlier history remarkable for their success in "winning souls," yet not a few have, in a quieter way, been instrumental in leading thousands to the happy experience of this great change; while the general clearness of discernment of the need of conversion, and the accurate teaching of the doctrine of conversion, have not fallen behind the teachings of earlier days to any serious degree, if at all. It is possible that in the greater breadth of labour which for some years has obtained, an equal concentration of attention on this central theme may have been wanting. The earlier appeals were made to a much greater extent than in later times to persons outside the Church, to the negligent and irreligious portion of the population; and in proportion as labour is expended upon such, the greater will be the number of obvious and striking conversions; whereas the calmer, quieter, and more gradual work amongst the families of the Church is equally blessed and real, if less observable in its character.

There has been no lowering of *the standard of the Christian character*, nor any abatement in the teaching of its permissible attainment, or its duteous pursuit. Wesley's great service to the Christian community rendered by his clear teaching of an exalted spiritual, but, at the same time, practical Christian life, has not to this hour been forgotten by "the people called Methodists." If the terms "perfection" and "perfect love" have not been used with the freedom with which in earlier times they were, the Christian ideal has not been reduced. Since the Wesleys themselves spake and sang of this "full redemption," the Connexion has not at any time had its attention so directly called to this subject, both by the press and other means, as within the past few years. And if some extravagances have impaired the teaching, they have evoked a more careful and discriminating correction. The effort to this day has been to raise the human life to higher and better conditions; higher in sanctity of thought and affection, higher in cultured religious sentiment, in devoutness of spirit, in loving, conscientious obedience to holy commandments; higher in charity and largeness of heart, in practical godliness, in service and Christian utility. Happily a part of the mission of Methodism has been fulfilled in the fact that surrounding Churches have caught the holy impulse, and now, far beyond the limits of Methodism, we hear the Methodist phrases, and behold to our joy the diffusion of the Methodist teaching with respect to this doctrine.

In one respect it may be thought that an essential part of the aim of Methodism has not, in this country at least, been attained to the degree that might have been expected. For several years it has been deplored that the number of *members in the Methodist Societies* has not kept adequate pace with the widespread and earnest activities, both ordinary and special, that have been maintained. This is a problem of extreme gravity, whose solution I am unable here to attempt. At the beginning of the century the membership in Great Britain was 90,619; to-day it is 420,982, with 59,887 in the preparatory junior classes. Considering the very widely extended and fervent efforts that have been put forth during the nine decades, it might have been expected that a much larger number would now be found enrolled; and the more so when it is considered that so large a number annually join the Society. I am not unmindful of the large secessions that have taken place, nor of the ill effects of those secessions upon the activities of the Connexion. One of the gravest problems for the consideration of future Methodism is how to retain in membership those who are once brought within its fold. But the *Christian communion*, for which the class-meeting, rightly conducted, presents such favourable opportunities, has not at any time been disowned; and recent attempts to give a wider comprehension to the Church have rendered it more obvious that the attachment of Methodism to its most honoured principle remains firm to this day.

The real nature of the communion demanded by the divine life, and the best methods of meeting those demands, have been more and more carefully studied. The essential features of the class-meeting it is seen may be preserved whilst some modifications of its methods are made. The testimony of Methodism to the necessity, the duty, and the privilege of individual and mutual service, to the right of every single member of the flock to the care and personal consideration, the sympathy and help of the other members, and the just demand of all upon each for his measure of service, has remained unaltered.[1] This is shown in the

---

[1] Abler indications of the scriptural character and practical value of this form of Christian fellowship have recently appeared, to one of which, in particular, I am glad to seize the opportunity of directing attention. I refer to the first of three prize Essays on "The Class-Meeting: A Defence and a Plea," by the Rev. William H. Thompson. See also previous Fernley Lectures by Rev. Dr. Gregory and W. F. Slater, M.A.

clear statements of the Annual Addresses of the Conference to the Societies, and in other official documents, and in the various publications issued by our Book-Room or by individual writers.

Passing from these features, which have more particular relation to those persons who hold an alliance with Methodism, to that which represents its attitude to the people outside its boundaries, I may inquire how far the Methodism of the past has been faithful to its original idea in respect of *evangelistic labour*. This has ever been the duty of Methodism to the world at large.

If the field-preaching has not been continued to the same extent as formerly, neither has it been abandoned. There has been nothing whatever to prevent, but everything to encourage, a frequent employment of outdoor preaching. If the demands of an elaborated Church organization have absorbed more attention than formerly, which must be acknowledged, they have not destroyed the evangelistic spirit, and most assuredly they have presented no real barrier to the freest evangelism. While it is of the utmost importance in order to promote the permanency and even the extension of Methodism, that the greatest care should be given to existing and established Churches, the prime work of Methodism is still amongst the ungodly.

It is true that we have had no single travelling evangelist like Wesley, but a general evangelistic spirit has been predominant amongst us; and to meet the growing necessities of the times, several ministers have for some years been devoted entirely to this work, without having the responsibilities of Circuit and pastoral duties.

That the multiplied activities of the pastorate which

recent years have brought must have interfered with the devotion of time and strength in the personal attention to many aggressive efforts, cannot be denied. Yet the spirit of Methodism to-day is such that he is the most acceptable and approved preacher whose labours largely assume this character. The heart of the people is set upon it, as is proved by the great interest manifested in Home Missionary work, the willing devotion of large gifts, and the ready consecration of time and service to it. This remark applies not merely to the more distinctively mission centres, but the same spirit pervades the Circuits from one end of the country to the other. Nothing wins greater sympathy from the whole body of the people than the exhibition of the old spirit of fervent evangelism. Nor are the ministers generally indifferent to this. In addition to those who are able to devote their energies to it, how many are there who would be thankful to embrace the opportunity of exchanging some of their necessary occupations for this most hallowed and blessed work!—men who have proved with Wesley, "We have a greater blessing in it than in any other work."

The greater demands upon the time and energies of the preachers made to-day by the almost complex arrangements for the general culture, instruction, and benefit of our people, together with the many religious and philanthropic activities—not to speak of more distracting occupations—found in connection with every congregation, have prohibited the appropriation of time many would gladly have given to evangelistic and expansive efforts. Moreover, the spirit of hesitation occasioned by the strong tides of questioning and sceptical unbelief which have rolled over the Churches during the later years, must have impaired the strength and absorbed the thoughts and time of many a preacher, and demanded an amount of energy in rebutting them which otherwise might have been spent in the more congenial and fruitful work of trying to convert the ungodly.

To how large an extent the sword has taken the place of the trowel! Men have been compelled to defend work already done, instead of seeking to win new possessions. The attention of much of the mind of the Church has been diverted from some of the more essential themes to others, which, if less fruitful of happy results and of far less permanent value, were for the time imperative. The faith of the Church may be finally confirmed by its successful combat with error in its ever-varying forms, but in the process time and energy are expended which are required to meet the necessities of the spiritually destitute and dying.

But both these kinds of service are of the highest importance. To scatter the clouds from the hearts of the doubting, equally with rescuing the depraved, is a true winning of souls. Often Methodism and Methodist workers are judged (all unconsciously it may be on the part of those who judge) by comparison with the brilliant examples of the great leaders of the past. In this is an element of unfairness. That Methodism has not produced another Wesley cannot be laid to it as a charge. If the Society of to-day be judged by the Society of past days, and the workers of to-day by the workers of the days gone by, although there may be less of adventure, less of the strong and constraining influence of widespread and exciting revival, less of the rugged boldness of men who were under little restraint from the keen eyes of a more sensitive and jealous public, there is also less demand for the severe and caustic corrections which Wesley felt himself compelled again and again to administer.

I will not abate a jot of the honour due to the men of former times, for their devoted zeal, their great service, their sanctity of character, their divinely honoured work; neither will I believe that in devotion to duty and fidelity to truth, in tone of character and singleness of aim, have my brethren, as a body, up to this day been a whit behind. I rejoice over those within the ministry, and the many noble-hearted men and women without, who have done, or are to-day doing service which arrests the eye and commands the admiration of an observant public; nor can I forget the equally noble, equally heroic, and more useful, if less prominent and less ostentatious, service of the great brotherhood of Methodist preachers throughout the land, and the great community of men and women, who in the common walks of life, in the hidden homes, and amid the ordinary activities of our Circuits, are engaged in a work as real, as deep, if not as novel, as the work done a hundred years ago.

It may be further inquired, How far has Methodism continued to exert an influence tending to "purify the Church," and, in an endeavour to spread scriptural holiness through the land, to provoke other labourers to jealousy?

It must be allowed that a very great change has taken place in the position of Methodism relatively to the Church of England. That in the earlier periods of its history it accomplished effectually, if not fully, the mission assigned to it in respect to the Church, has been ungrudgingly acknowledged and affirmed by many. To a Methodist source must be traced the great revival of pure and fervent religion in the Church of England, which I venture to characterise as one of the most pleasing signs of our national life to-day. But inasmuch as we have had no representatives within its borders, no Wesley, or Fletcher, or Whitefield to speak in the pulpits, and no clergymen amongst the ranks of the "travelling preachers" (such an arrangement being no longer possible), whatever measure of influence could be exerted by Methodism upon the Church could be exerted only *from without*. But it is not difficult to see that in various ways that influence may have been continued. In as far as purity of doctrine, the proprieties of Christian worship, the fidelities of godly living, and the fervour of Christian activities are exhibited by any Church, they cannot but be beneficial to all the other Churches around. By how much Methodism has maintained a faithful exhibition of these qualities, by so much has it exerted a silent influence for good upon the Church out of which it sprang. One source of what I hope has been beneficent service is to be found in the number of Methodists who have annually passed from Methodism to the Church, an incidental mode of carrying on its original purpose of leavening the Church; but though this has been the case from the beginning of the century, I can scarcely be persuaded to rejoice in the fact.

In one respect, alas! Methodism has been compelled to assume an attitude of dissent and even of antagonism towards the Church; and it is to the great grief of many of her ministers and people that it has been driven to do so.

Even those who to-day have the most loving regard for the Church of the Reformation (still to be regarded as such, notwithstanding that some of her own sons repudiate the title, and others, being unfaithful to the supreme authority of Holy Scripture, are unfaithful to Reformation principles); who thankfully acknowledge her inestimable service to Christian literature, fruit of the scholarship and sanctified talent which have ever been found in her ranks; who appreciate the spiritual beauties of her liturgy, the godly zeal of so many of her clergy, the cultured Christian life and useful Christian service of thousands of her people, the forceful moral influence exerted by her upon English society, and the honourable position she occupies amongst the Churches of Christendom,—even they are driven, though mournfully, to an attitude of opposition, by what appears to them to be a departure, both in doctrinal teaching and in details of liturgical worship, from the simplicity of the gospel and from the Church's own best and earliest writings.

It cannot be expected that Methodism could stand in any other than a position of separation, and even of protest, in respect to a Church whose officers claim the priestly function of absolution; who make the memorial of the Lord a renewal or "extension" of His sacrifice; who deny grace to a sacrament administered by other hands than those of an exclusive order, ordained by claimants to a direct descent from the apostles, who interpret the initiatory rite in the Church, the pledge of discipleship and the covenant pledge of grace, as an actual conveyance of regenerating grace: and so long as Methodism holds to the absolute supremacy of Holy Scripture, this attitude cannot be changed. The especial force of the testimony of Methodism against these assumptions is to be found in the fact that equal proofs of spiritual regeneration and sanctity of life have appeared under its ministrations without these adjuncts. Pure and exalted Christian life in Methodism has been and still is its dignified and effective witness against these pretensions. It has been given to it in company with the other non-conforming Churches to declare the independence of the true spiritual kingdom of all such mere externals. It is a part of its calling, as it has been from the beginning, to witness to the great truth that the real ends of the Christian teaching, the ends of Church activity and organization, may be attained, men and women may be rescued from the barren wastes of sinful degradation, Christian character may be cultured, and Christian philanthropy and charity, self-denial and self-sacrifice developed, without the aid of the elaborated service, without the pretensions of Rome, without the ceremonial, the apostolical succession, or the intervention of priests, without the dogmas of transubstantiation, the real presence, or baptismal regeneration. The plain historic testimony of Methodism is to the non-necessity for episcopal ordination with these appendages, in order to the gathering of sinners to Christ, in order to the conversion of the ungodly, or the culture of the spiritual life.

It has been said that, inasmuch as Wesley did not desire to remove from the Church, and seeing that the Church is now so greatly changed in spiritual character and activity, Methodism ought to return, that the new may be grafted upon the old. Apart from the fact that though a twig may be ingrafted, it is not easy to ingraft a tree, it must be asked in reply, Has the Church so far changed as to render the distinctive witness needless? We do not so believe. Would that it were so! It is impossible to express our thankful joy at the greatly altered condition of the Church; but in presence of the prevalent arrogant assumptions of priestly clergy, in whose view we are no Church, neither is there any outside the borders of the Episcopal, and the rejection of the authority of Holy Scripture by others, Methodism must remain to bear its witness that the theory is illusory. With a deep, heart-felt sorrow at beholding the many rents in the outer garment of Christ, we cannot, we dare not, any more than our fathers dared, merge our work in one which, as we believe, directly contradicts, in these particulars, the spirit, the genius, the historic record of the Church, and above all the voice of the sacred word, and which, as we are equally persuaded, bases these assumptions on a false foundation. It is a great Church in this land, and we are relatively but a little people. It has its hold in many ways upon the higher ranks of English society, and a widespread and well-deserved influence over a larger number of our English people than any other Church; and we have our hand only on some of the less wealthy and less influential; but though our numbers be smaller and our external influence feebler, we must raise our voice and bear our testimony even by what is, to some of us at least, a painful separation.

If Methodism presented no examples of a cultured Christian life, or of true Christian zeal and fervent charity, this testimony would be powerless. But we are able to point not merely to individual instances of Christian goodness, but to multiplied Churches which bring to our view, and to the view of the world, the abundant fruits of godliness. These at least are the seals to our ministry, and the indubitable vindication of the justness and the reality of the position we now assume.

In the earlier days of Methodism a distinctive part of its calling was affirmed to be *to supply the lack of service of the existing clergy*; and the question may well be proposed, How far has this been done up to the present time? Alas! it would appear that the whole work of all the Churches, notwithstanding that it has been so greatly increased in the past few decades, has been hitherto insufficient to meet adequately the necessities of the country. There are still areas of unblessed, unalleviated spiritual destitution; and there are masses of the people who are yet unreclaimed.

There need be little jealousy amongst the workers where every one may be employed in holy rivalry to do the work which the united energies of all fail to overtake. Happily in many a parish the pure gospel has been and still is preached, while the beautiful proprieties of public worship, which present so striking a contrast to the cold carelessness of the earlier part of the century, now lure the feet of the worshippers into a sanctuary where they are not fed with mere husks. And in many of our large towns we have rejoicingly witnessed the increased labours of a devoted clergy (not to speak of the ministers and workers in other Churches) sometimes putting us to the blush by their unwearied and toilsome service.

How many whom we once provoked to jealousy by our more abundant labour have been able to turn round upon us with corrective glance, bidding us to emulate their fervent and self-denying work! Here there was little need for us to supply their "lack of service." We have seen services multiplied, both on the Sabbath and weekdays, in happy imitation of our fathers' methods, and novel ones introduced which had long been commonplaces with us. The area is being limited over which we have to mourn the absence of faithful labourers. False motives may have been attributed to active curates whose quick foot was heard in slums and alleys and garrets, or in the homes of cottage-labourers; but there is no contradicting the fact, nor do we wish to contradict it, that the awakened zeal of the English clergy to-day presents one of the brightest aspects of the Church's condition.

But the work of Methodism is not rendered unnecessary even where its methods have been adopted or its spirit breathed by others. Even where the old parish church might seem to afford ample accommodation for all the worshippers, and the labours of the clergy appear to be sufficient to meet the requirements of all the people dwelling within the parochial limits, it must be confessed that in many places what appears to us to be an imperfect and often a false teaching, and in others a "broad" but not deep conception of scriptural sanctity, demand the presence of the apparently obtrusive "travelling preacher."

To spread "scriptural holiness over the land" has ever been, and ever must be, a distinctive feature of the calling of Methodism. In constructing the phrase, "scriptural holiness," Wesley had in mind the unscriptural views so widely spread abroad; and his followers since his day have been driven to have respect to the same.

I do not think that Methodism up to this day has need to fear being judged in presence of the original purpose and design of its existence. It is impossible without a thrill of gratitude to refer to the many direct and determined efforts to grapple with the spiritual destitution and apathy still to be found in our midst; to provide services which shall prove to be attractive even to the neglecters of public worship; to the diversifying of the ordinary methods of pastoral duty in order to meet the special social conditions of particular areas of population. While all the work of Methodism in this country has from the beginning been defined as a home-mission work, and every minister has been taught to look upon himself as a home missionary, yet with a view to meet these special necessities which ordinary Circuit arrangements do not reach, a special Home-Mission agency has for many years been in active and successful operation, varying in its methods to meet varying needs, and varying in its success through many causes.[1]

Since the year 1857, a very active propaganda of this kind has been carried on, which during the last few years, aided by specially qualified men, has expanded to proportions and has been distinguished by a courage and crowned with a success that have excited the astonishment and admiration of observant Churches around. It is equally pleasing to see so many men of special qualifications raised up amongst us who are ready to undertake this pioneer work, and at the same time to mark the enthusiasm with which they are sustained by our people.

[1] See Resolutions of the Conference on Home Missions. *Minutes*, 1855, 1856.

This work is being commenced in many of our large towns. Depleted congregations are being resuscitated. Old sanctuaries, once the scenes of great spiritual achievements, hallowed to many a family by the most sacred associations, by memories of cherished friendships, and of early efforts of Christian service, and by many other ties of an endearing and enduring kind, but which are either abandoned by a retiring population or desolated through the many causes for change now so powerfully at work in the centres of our growing cities, are being seized upon as affording the most suitable spheres for fresh endeavours, and are already appearing in the beauty of renewed life.

All this is in keeping with the early calling to "go not only to those who want you, but to those who want you most." And the work is being carried on in a way and by classes of workers which give promise of permanent benefit to many a dark and destitute district.

Nor has Methodism been indifferent to the great *social problems* of the day, some of which have pressed for solution. In my own opinion there is a far more careful and well-regulated effort made to-day, modified by the many changed external conditions, but not in any degree less searching or effective, than was put forth in the best times of the past.

I have spoken of Wesley as the embodiment of his own system. It finds its highest illustration in him. With lofty views of the possibilities of the individual life, he combined wide sympathies with the life of the community, and laboured hard to promote its welfare. He endeavoured to ameliorate social conditions, even the lowest, as when he visited the prisons and aided poor debtors; or when he established "a lending stock" to help struggling tradesmen and to set up others in business; or provided cheap literature of a wholesome kind to meet the wants of cottage-labourers and of the poor, publishing poetry, and history, and science, and general reading, and even music; or when he opened schools for the ignorant, or founded dispensaries for the sick, or placed the four electrical machines in different parts of London, that they who could not afford to pay for the benefit of what he and many others believed to be a powerful remedial agent, might have it gratuitously; or when he strove by his tracts to correct smuggling and bribery, and "street walking" and other common vices; or taught his people to care for the poor and the suffering by his truly Christ-like "Strangers' Friend Society;" or by his Orphanage at Newcastle he sought to rescue the exposed youth. Methodism could not, at any time be called Wesleyan if it did not follow him in these works. I think it must now be judged to have been not unfaithful in these matters even to its best traditions. With a prudent avoidance of entanglement in the strife of party politics, there has been no lack of interest in the great movements for the welfare of the community which as a Christian Church it could take part in. With its views of the individual life, it could not have a low estimate of the family or the national life, or of its duty to aid in their progress. At considerable outlay of money, and by the expenditure of much talent, education, in its lower, middle-class, and higher departments, has received careful consideration. The circulation of pure literature has been continued. Care for the poor, and especially the waifs and strays of society, has been displayed in its model Children's Homes and Orphanages; while temperance, Sabbath observance, and social purity have been promoted. And the many questions affecting the relations and mutual interests of different classes of the community, the general welfare of the poor, the sanitation of their houses, harmless and improving recreations, have not escaped attention.

Methodism must needs leave many questions of great, if of subsidiary importance, to others. If the proportion of attention given to some of the great problems which await discussion may seem to be small in comparison with that which some other Churches have been able to give, it must be borne in mind that Methodism was raised up for special ends; and while not indifferent to these pressing questions, it would be false and faithless to a high calling were its attention diverted or its energies engrossed by secondary topics. Its one supreme calling is to do *spiritual service;* its chief strength has always been in its spiritual aim. It is abundantly a worthy calling. If stated with the utmost baldness as a calling to save souls, it is still a high calling. It is our first, our chiefest, our best work. It has been our crown of rejoicing, and we should add no honour to ourselves by disowning it. We do not disown it: we glory in it, and our glorying is not vain. It is the work in which our fathers strove to be most laborious, in which they won most laurels, and by which they best served their race.

We have seen that the Divine Providence, which "thrust out" the two brothers Wesley, against their will, "to raise up a holy people" in this land, drew out the sympathies of the entire Connexion without its anticipation to raise up holy peoples in fields far remote; and we have seen how a community, trained by fervent teaching and by holy song to a belief in "the redemption of the world by our Lord Jesus Christ," and in the suitableness of the gospel as a message to the outlying populations of the earth as truly as to the inhabitants of this land; trained, moreover, to entertain a wide and tender sympathy with the world, and to the habit of willing service and free contributions for benevolent objects, entered with energy and holy zeal into the purposes of a revived Church; and, hearing the cries of the needy, gave of its sons and its means to carry the glad message to the ends of the earth. *Foreign Missions*, which have been since the days of Wesley one of the chief honours of Methodism, continue to be its most cherished institution. Its Missionary Society has held, and still holds, a foremost place amongst similar societies of the land. In no work has Methodism been more faithful to the high calling of God than in the maintenance of these missions. In no work does it take a deeper interest to-day.

I have more than once, when using the term Methodist, designed it to represent all the communities that bear that name—the total idea of Methodism in the world. It would not be improper to ask, How far has Methodism, as a whole, been faithful to the original aim?

I am not disposed to depart from the final definition of our calling, already given, even though it includes the words, "not to found a new sect." The "Methodist New Connexion" was the first to break the unity of the

Society. I do not question either the *bona fides* of men of that day in contending for principles, some of which, though then judged to be premature by the older Connexion, are now incorporated in it; but I must say that I wish they who separated from us had remembered Wesley's words, "not to found a new sect." Any real necessity for that sect did not, in my judgment, exist.[1] Since its formation, however, the little company has wrought hard, and has attained to a position of influence in the country. It has always striven to accomplish the same ends as the parent body, and has always been faithful to Methodist doctrine.

The two bodies continued to labour on side by side until another separation took place, different from the former. I allude to the "Primitive Methodists." Of this humble and hard-working Society it must be said that, according to its means, it has steadily and faithfully endeavoured to carry out the true aims of Methodism. And if the structure of its Church organization does not commend itself to our approval, it is impossible not to admire the fervent zeal and widespread usefulness by which its activities have ever been characterized. It has never swerved from the true doctrines or true aim of Methodism.

The Bible Christians followed in much the same path of earnest if restricted service.

In Ireland the old Methodist principle so far prevailed

---

[1] "Mr. Kilham might have rendered good service to Methodism by suggesting modifications and expansions of a system, the history of which up to that moment had been that of a series of skilful modifications and of expansions carefully conceived and carefully carried out," etc. etc.—(*Handbook of Methodism*, Dr. Gregory.) The Handbook also shows that much more was contended for by Mr. Kilham than the Methodist New Connexion accepted.

that, when it was determined to have service in Church hours, and to administer the Lord's Supper, about one-half of the Society seceded and became the "Church Methodists" or "Primitive Wesleyans" of Ireland. On the disestablishment of the Irish Church they rejoined us. For the formation of two other sects, the Wesleyan Association and the Wesleyan Methodist Reformers, I can find no sufficient justification. When thinking of them, and of some other smaller offshoots, the words of Wesley rise again and again to my mind, "not to form another sect."

Putting aside, however, the question of separation, I hesitate not to say that these several sections of Methodism have retained, some in greater and some in less degree, its original spirit and purpose, have been faithful to its doctrinal standards, and, except in times of strife and agitation, have aimed at the accomplishment, by various ways, of the original and essential purpose of Methodism.

But what shall be said of the effect of these divisions? Surely the strength of Methodism, and its influence in the nation, have suffered greatly by this sundering of it into parties and sects; nor does it appear to me that any adequate and compensating gain has been made, while it cannot be doubted that it was entirely opposed to Wesley's own expressed wish. In addition to considerable losses of members from the original Society (amounting in the last agitation to no less than 100,000, a portion only of whom could be gathered up by the separating Churches), great injury was occasioned to the working of Methodism; its progressive activities were for a time arrested, and its public appearance greatly impaired.

If mention is made of the various foreign offshoots of

Methodism, all of which are to be classed under the one name, the first to arrest attention is the American Episcopal Church. It stands pre-eminent, alike on account of its being the first founded in point of time, the peculiar circumstances attending its institution, and its surprising growth, numbers, and influence.

I shall content myself here with a testimony which will, I am sure, be received with the utmost respect in this country. On the occasion of a visit of the late Dean Stanley to America, a reception was given to him by the Methodists of New York, when he spoke of Methodism in that kind and generous spirit which characterized him. In replying to his address, Bishop Simpson referred to the marking out by Wesley of the great outlines of the movement which they, in part, represented, and said: "Near the close of his long life he advised the formation of a Church according to the order which we now have; and there is no other organization or communion on earth which so clearly and distinctly represents the mind of John Wesley as the organization of the Methodist Episcopal Church. He planned its order, and we simply followed his advice."[1]

The Canadian and other colonial Churches have sprung from our missionary efforts, and retain the characteristics of the parent stem. In doctrine, in the important place assigned to conversion and to Christian fellowship, in the insistence on holiness and in a true evangelism, in the maintenance of the Connexional principle and the terms of Church membership, these, with small abatement, have adhered faithfully to the original type. Nor need I omit

[1] Daniels, *A Short History of the Methodists*, p. 186.

the Calvinistic branch of "the great revival," especially as represented in the large and flourishing Calvinistic Methodist Churches of the Principality.

If this review be just, Methodism at this hour stands free from any serious charge of departure from the original design and mission for which Wesley believed it to be raised up. It is very pleasing to stand in the present hour, after the celebration of the third jubilee of the Society's existence, and a century after the death of its founder, and to be able to affirm its general adhesion, throughout the changing years, to its original calling and mission. With a prudent adaptation in the details of external form to the ever-varying requirements of the era, Methodism is essentially as it was when it left the hands of Wesley. Changes have been made, not in opposition to its essential principles, but with the design of carrying out more efficiently its avowed purpose.

"From year to year, and from generation to generation, the same unity of aim and concentration of effort have been preserved. There have been changes in Methodism, though these have been gradually made; but the Methodists are to-day in the same spirit and resolution as they were in the days of John Wesley. They have never sought to weaken the influence or attract to themselves the members of other Churches, but they have, with untiring perseverance, set themselves to extend the power of their own. They have achieved the success which seldom fails to reward earnest devotion to a great object, when it has at its command such force as the Society has always been able to supply."[1]

---

[1] Rogers, p. 551. See Appendix E.

CHAPTER IV.

THE RELATION OF METHODISM TO THE FUTURE.

Has Methodism still a Mission? If so, what?

ANOTHER branch of our inquiry now opens before us. We have seen that Methodism had a definite calling in the past, and a mission clearly defined and very impressive. Does that call continue? or is the end for which Methodism was raised up answered? Is its work finished? Is its mission fulfilled? Does anything remain to be done by Methodism in advancing that general progress of the race which it was designed to promote? Is it to-day fitted to do any important work; or has its strength been exhausted? Is it effete—a spent force? Is it unnecessary and therefore useless, and, if useless, injurious? Would it therefore be for the world's advantage to remove it out of the way? Can the old ship be used no longer? Does she leak? Are the sails torn and the spars broken past mending? Must the poor battered old hull now be moored into quiet waters, an interesting memorial of an interesting past, but having no adaptation to present needs; useless, worthless, done with; save that this, like another flagship, remains a pleasing relic of a bygone time, suitable only to amuse holiday-makers?

Do you believe it? Does any one really believe it who

has taken any pains to consider the question? I know that some persons would say—have said with glib lip—that Methodism has had its day. Its day indeed! My own belief is that such an assertion can only be made in carelessness, or indifference, if not from more unworthy impulses. Methodism has seen the bright rays of the morning's light, and felt the crisp sharpness of the morning air. It has risen with the sun. But the perfect day of Methodism lies in the future. Loving the past as I do, reading it as a beautiful spiritual epic full of thrilling incident, delighting, exulting in it, I yet believe that the possibilities of Methodism for usefulness in the world to-day far outstrip those of any previous period of its history. If the sons of Methodism are faithful to their calling, they may do a work for the future of their race which shall in no wise be shamed by the wonderful works of the past.

But let us suppose that the question is really presented in all seriousness, *Has Methodism still a mission on the earth?* Methodism a mission! What is the answer of the 2,000 ministers enrolled within its ranks, or of the 500,000 members embraced within its closest fellowship? of its army of leaders and local preachers and Sabbath-school teachers? What is the answer of the vast Churches of England, of America, and Canada, and the growing Churches of Australia and South Africa? Methodism a mission! With its sanctuaries in every town and almost every village; its schools and colleges and high-class educational institutions; with its history adorned by noble lives of self-denial and useful service to encourage and instruct future generations, and the experiments of many methods to guide in future endeavours; with the experience of a hundred and fifty years of work which has proved a blessing and an inspiration to universal Protestantism; with its vantage ground for labour, not in England alone, where it covers areas which from supineness or untoward circumstances had been so long neglected, but in the wider sphere of the world where its ramifications are so extended; with its affiliated Conferences established in the great centres of colonial life, and an occupancy of fields of heathendom such as no Church exceeds; with its measure of influence in this country, and its care for the nations of the earth, and its adaptation to meet the spiritual wants of men, in which it is not outstripped by any of the Churches; with its means of grace and methods of service and its system of Church government that are easily adapted to the diversities of national character, habits, and susceptibilities; with a position of honour and respect and happy fellowship amongst the Churches, not one of which but owes to it a debt of gratitude for the highest spiritual service; with no cause for quarrel or rivalry subsisting between it and them save the holy rivalry of seeking which can do the greatest amount of good in the world!

Is the *raison d'être* of a Church gone that needs no addition in order to make it in the future, what it has proved itself to be in the past, an efficient agency for the extension of the kingdom of God on the earth? Or is there such a plethora of Christian workers to-day that this one can be easily spared? Can the work that is needed in this and in other lands be done without the aid of Methodism? Are the other Churches capable of doing it? Is not the work here and abroad greater than we can all do? If a justification is demanded for the continuance of Methodism, we must reply, What could justify its destruction? The one demand must be met by the other. As one of the many spiritual forces in the world, its continuance is necessitated by the world's condition. What would be the gain to Christianity were Methodism blotted out to-day? Is Methodism a stain on the page of the Church's history? Has it been recreant to the true spirit, or just aims, or false to the doctrines and teaching of Christianity? Would the Reformation Churches of this land have their hands strengthened by the removal of Methodism? Let these questions be answered. Does it hinder other Churches in their work, and therefore must it be set aside? Can it be spared? Can any of the other Churches be spared? No; not one. The world needs the whole of them. Its cry is heard for every helper and every agency. Four-sevenths of the world's inhabitants are to-day in the darkness of heathendom. Is this a time to be harking back? So far is Christianity from universal diffusion that there is an imperative demand for every effort to keep pace with the growing populations of the earth. In view of the world's need, Christianity is too weak a force in the earth to allow of the withdrawal of a single agent, or the abatement of a single effort. This line of argument is certainly legitimate.

The Divine Providence which raised up Methodism has put a signal token of blessing and approval upon it. Only by unfaithfulness could the great calling become other than an abiding obligation. False friends or cruel enemies may deny to Methodism a place and a mission in the earth; but the Divine Hand, which imposed the first heavy burden of responsibility upon it, has not uplifted that burden. The call to continue its work is as clear, and the necessity for its labour is as pressing, as when the same Divine Providence "thrust out" its first leaders "to raise up a holy seed." If men outside Methodism, or any within, whose love is growing cold, deny the need of this evangelizing force in the world to-day, the men who are faithful to the divine purpose hear distinctly the call of duty to fulfil a mission which widens as the times roll by. The position occupied by Methodism to-day is the loudest call to fidelity to a mission which only such a position could impose. Are we asked to abandon Methodism? We say as Wesley said, "We cannot do this with a safe conscience; for we apprehend many souls would be lost thereby, and that God would require their blood at our hands."[1]

It is not for the Methodist Church to ask an onlooking world in its supineness, or any outside its own boundary, whether the commission of Divine Providence is withdrawn. There is but one place where this inquiry must be presented, or where the response to this demand can be heard. The oracle is within the temple. In the secret and sacred depths of the Methodist conscience alone must the pleading request be uttered, or the reply be received. There only can the voice be heard which calls for holy service and makes its neglect a crime. If any chilling fear ever crept, or creeps, over the hearts of John Wesley's followers, "the people called Methodists," that their work is done, their commission withdrawn, their duty at an end, their mission closed, the first imperative demand must be whether it is by its complete fulfilment, or by its withdrawal through unfaithfulness. It can only be by the thoughtful, prayerful,

[1] *Works*, vol. i. p. 487.

Relation of Methodism to the Future. 169

intent communion with the indwelling Spirit, by the faithful searching of heart, the humility which means a tremulous sensibility to divine conviction, that any answer to so grave a question can be gained. To seek a reply at the hands of a frivolous or unfriendly onlooker would be recreant to a divine command. Having once heard the authoritative voice calling to labour, it would be but a guilty tampering with duty to require the reiteration of the command.

Did the conscience of the Connexion need to be reawakened to the solemnity of the call of God, or had conviction paled before difficulties, or become feeble through inaction, then the suitable word of reawakening would be a word to each individual Methodist to search and try his own heart, and estimate his own labour, and fathom his own duty in presence of the world in its need, and (with the uttermost solemnity) in presence of the God of all grace. The mission of Methodism as a whole is made up of the distinct mission of each individual member; for it is one of the essential features of Methodism that it gives each a recognised position, and each a responsible work. Methodism has a partial force as an idea; but it is comparatively inappreciable in presence of the force of the combined energy of the individual members of its community. Fidelity or unfaithfulness is not the fidelity or unfaithfulness of a mass, but of individuals.

The birth of Methodism into the world marks an epoch in the spiritual history of the race which will never be forgotten. Its agents may be negligent, though I do not think that they are or will be; but were they to become so, the onlookers would take up the weapons which their idle hands had laid down. Should all its institutions lie as ruins, they would, like the ruins of old Greece and Rome, be everlasting models on which following ages would frame their ideas.

Methodism may not be adapted to meet the preferences of the people of this country generally. The constant loss of its members may seem to point to this. It may lack the necessary comprehensiveness. It is worthy of consideration whether it is adapted or designed to meet these wide demands. It may be no calling of Methodism to be so. But that it is a great moral force in the empire cannot be ignored. The Methodist need not be ashamed of his Methodism, albeit many outside place little value on it, or deride it on account of its eccentricities, seeing, it may be, only its less necessary features, and overlooking its essential ones.

Standing in the present and looking forward to the hastily coming future, it may be asked, What is the immediate duty incumbent upon the Methodist Churches? What is the mission of Methodism as interpreted at this hour? In what way does it appear that it can best meet the needs of the future? Any answer that I may give to this question must be prefaced by this general statement, that the mission of Methodism to-day is the same as its mission in the beginning. If Methodism would render its best and utmost service to the world, it must be by maintaining a close fidelity to its original principles, and to the employment of its original methods. *The true programme for the future lies in the past.* Even the changed conditions of social life call for little more than a slight readjustment of details. To lead men to conviction of sin and to conversion from it, to guide them to holiness of life, to Christian fellowship and Christian activity and in the ministries of Christian charity to care for the unconverted mass of our fellow-countrymen, and for the unenlightened nations of the earth, are primal duties. There may be a constant provocation to jealousy, a continual attempt to supply the lack of service; a ceaseless endeavour to spread scriptural holiness over the land. It is needful to do these things, and to do them in our old way, even though there is not so great a deficiency of like work by other Churches now as formerly.

Of course Methodism has its mission, in common with all the other Churches, in seeking the general uplifting of English society; and the fidelity of every Church is demanded by a needy, sinful, suffering world. Without denying the special adaptation of the several Churches to accomplish special ends of great practical importance, there must be recognised a common call to aid in promoting the general progress. All may strive to promote the true dignity of life and the sanctity of service, the purity of home, the joys of religion, the holiness of labour, the character and contagion of charity, and whatever tends to beautify and adorn human life. All may teach truthfulness, honour, sobriety, neighbourly love, pitiful consideration of the needy and sinful. It is the part of every company of disciples of the common Lord to throw light upon life and immortality, to make the one look more beauteous and the other more real and attractive. It is part of the calling of every Church to draw men to the preparation for endless life, to the sanctity which prepares for it, and which makes it a necessity.

To aid in the accomplishment of this general work, Methodism takes its place in the community of the Churches, *finding its own special mission now to be partially, perhaps to a great extent, but not wholly, merged in this common work of the Christian Churches of the world*, of which work it gladly takes its share. One of the greatest tasks of the present hour is to get at the vast multitudes of the people who are outside all our Churches, and make them the captives of the love of God.

We do not, we cannot arrogate to ourselves an ability or a special adaptation to meet all the requirements of the hour; but we have our own work, our special work, and our share of the common work. Are our methods adapted to the duty imposed upon us? If Methodism has but to do a part of the great work of the Churches, and in conjunction with them, so be it. That work is most honourable and glorious, and the calling to help in it is an honourable and glorious calling. If Methodism has not a mission for which it is specially fitted, then the justification for its continuance falls upon the same plane with that of the other Churches of the land. But there are *distinctive features* in Methodism, features which differentiate it from all the Churches. The real justification of Methodism lies in the suitability and efficiency of its special methods to promote the high end of all the Churches. For illustrations of this, it may be sufficient to turn back to its past history; to the great spiritual revolution effected through its instrumentality in this country; to its beneficent influence upon all the existing Churches of the land, as acknowledged by an abundance of independent testimonies; to its almost unequalled work in the United States of America and in Canada; to its extended influence in many lands of the earth. These are sufficient evidence of its adaptability to accomplish great ends by its own special means, even apart from any estimate of those means themselves.

Let it then be acknowledged that Methodism takes its place amongst the sisterhood of Churches. Whether it is worthy so to do or not, I will not argue here. Assuredly, without hesitation, I may presume it to be so. It has then a mission in common with the whole—a mission to preach, to gather into Christian fellowship, to develop Christian character, to cultivate morality, to exhibit Christian charity, to seek to reclaim the wandering and wicked, and to proclaim the gospel to the nations of the earth—the common aims of all Christian communities.

But has Methodism any distinctive mission? or is its work bounded by the general work of the Churches? I think it is not difficult to see that while Methodism has its work, perhaps its chief work, in the common work of the Churches, it has also a particular and special work to do.

Placing ourselves in alliance with the early workers in Methodism, we see that the condition of the moral life of the country, and the state of the Churches at the time, did assuredly demand the upraising of a specialized agency to do a special work. That work was done in a most effective manner, as all the Churches to-day acknowledge. The work begun with very clearly defined purposes has been continued to the present time. It has, however, it must be confessed, assumed a character which in some respects differs from that of the original work. But it is as the difference between the root of a tree and its branches and leaves and fruit. The present Methodism has grown out of the early Methodism, and is one with it. But the external conditions have changed. The state of the Churches and of religion generally in the country has undergone a great transformation, and mainly as the result of the Methodist revival. Methodism itself, too, has changed, both in respect of its relation to the Established Church and in respect of its own organization, which has become more settled and elaborated. It cannot be said in any way to have changed in its principles and aims. It is mainly in its relation to its environment that the Methodism of to-day differs from that of the last century. I do not think that it could be said that there is to-day the need for an organization that would stand in precisely the same relation to the Established Church as Methodism stood to it in its earlier years. The times have changed: the relations of contemporary Societies have changed. The spiritual deadness has passed away which a hundred and fifty years ago called for the interposition of some agency whose influence should be directed to awaken and restore to life and activity. The revival, " the memorable Methodist revival,"[1] has taken place. It is distinguished as " The Religious Revival,"[2] " The Evangelical Revival of the eighteenth century."[3] Over that revival we all rejoice. It continues to this day. If we cannot with minuteness trace the subsequent revival of the present century in the English Church to it (although the links are not altogether wanting, as has been most clearly shown[4]), yet, without contradiction, the former paved the way for the latter, was its precursor, if not, indeed, its very cause. The religious revival of the eighteenth century bears its fruit

---

[1] Stoughton. [2] Lecky. [3] Overton. [4] Stoughton.

in the nineteenth. The fields which then were barren and arid are now covered with verdure. Whatever the English Churches need to-day, they do not need that reawakening into life and activity which was the great necessity when Methodism arose, and to effect which it was the chosen instrument. Nor can it be said that there is the same need to bring to light hidden and half-forgotten doctrinal truths. The great verities it was Wesley's honoured mission to unveil and to proclaim to a forgetful Church and an ignorant world are now common-places in the Churches.

Even the agencies which Wesley first called into play are active powers to-day on every hand; and the demand for individual service, which he laid upon every believer as a duty, is acknowledged and responded to by whole armies of willing and zealous soldiers in the great campaign.

Whether the "purifying of the Church" has been accomplished to the degree contemplated by him, whether there has been as abundant a supply of "the lack of service," or whether the "provocation to jealousy" was as effectual as he designed, we need not now determine. But who can doubt that the jealousy was provoked, that the lack of service was according to ability supplied, or that the purifying both of doctrine and of life in the Church was effected to a very large degree?

It is not an extravagance to speak of the present time as fraught with great issues. Looking out upon the wide fields of the national life, it is impossible to avoid being arrested by the feverish heat and haste observable in many departments of human activity. Changes very great, and some of them very rapid, are being made in the social and political spheres. Forces are at work tending greatly to alter the relative positions of different sections of English society. There is a holy ferment of excitement and activity amongst the Churches. There is a strong conflict of opinion on the most important Christian verities, and on some of them a very serious assault is being made. Important social questions are claiming public attention. We are not escaping the effect of the great socialistic movement of the Continent, which at present is like a shifting, uncontrollable sandbank; nor the opening of nation to nation, the dispersion of large portions of the surplus populations both of the Eastern and Western world, driven out from their homes by the necessities of trade, or drawn by the alluring prospect of gain.

The Churches of to-day are amongst the seers for the race. To discern with quick eye the upspringing of new sources of danger to the moral and social life of the people, the appearance of any darkening cloud of error, or the presence of new forces available for the promotion of the general well-being, and to hasten forward to arrest those and prudently to direct these, is a duty of a very pressing character.

These conditions will not take the leaders of Methodism by surprise. A steady outlook over the wide fields of national, and the wider fields of the universal life, is maintained. And it has hitherto been the wisdom of its leaders to adapt its methods to the necessities of the hour; and although it must be quite beyond the power of Methodism, as, indeed, it is of any single community, even the greatest, to deal alone with the many problems which present themselves for solution, yet it will be the duty, and I am persuaded it will be the effort, of the Connexion in the future, as it has been in the past, to strive to do its share of the great work which imposes itself upon all who charge themselves with the responsibility of caring for the spiritual interests of mankind.

What now remains to be done? What is the immediate and pressing call of the hour upon Methodism ? and how far is it fitted to answer to that call ? What is the present clarion cry ?

I have suggested that we are to find in the past the inspiration and the guidance for the future. I repeat this by saying that we need no new Methodism, no new spirit or aim or method. The truer we are to our original principles, the more we can catch the spirit of our fathers, the more steadily we can hold before us the same definite designs, and the more faithfully we cling to their methods, the more effectually shall we, in the future, carry on the great work which they so nobly and so well began.

I have named four characteristics that distinguished Methodism at its outset, and I have suggested it to have been the great calling of our fathers—the early Methodists—to give prominence to these. To give pre-eminence to the same four features is the calling of Methodism in the future. This is our peculiar mission. We have our duty in common with the Evangelical Churches of this and other lands, but a special adaptation to special service imposes upon us special obligations. And first, of conversion. This is the point at which we began. We are ever to recur to it—its clear definition ; its imperative necessity. It must be urged as at the first, and on the same grounds. Sin must be shown to be sin, even exceeding sinful. It is not in harmony with the doctrinal teaching of Methodism to abate the evilness of wrong-doing or of wrong-being. Its terrible consequences must not be hidden. Those consequences are not rendered less terrible by changes in theory concerning the future punishments of sin. A definite, unmistakeable assertion of the old alternatives must be made: "Except ye repent, ye shall all likewise perish." "Except a man be born anew, he cannot see the kingdom of God."

There is a danger of this teaching being overlooked or weakened, in the tendency to narrow preaching to a cultivation of certain elements of Christian character; or even to turn off to consider social and semi-political subjects. There are times and places for these subjects. They need not be ignored; but they must not take front rank, or force the primary questions aside. This kind of preaching must not usurp the pulpits of Methodism. Its first glory wanes, its subsequent work is withered, if the great truth be not first, "Ye must be born again." It is impossible to exaggerate the importance of this. Let us promote moral culture by all means; but first let us aim at the quickening of the moral life. A soul reawakened by the Divine Spirit, brought by a sincere repentance, and by a living faith in the Saviour, to a consciousness of reconciliation with God, and to the happy exultation in the experience of a new spiritual life, is capable of the utmost delicacy of moral culture; it is as plastic clay under the fingers of the modeller, and becomes a fount of all godly living, all Christian service, all holy charity.

Conversion is a first principle with us. By how much we depart from a direct insistence on it, by so much is our distinctive mission impaired. Every one of all the great subsidiary questions must be kept before our minds; but this is subsidiary to none.

I have illustrated the essential features of our system by a reference to the personal history of our founder. Here was one set upon the pursuit of holiness, hungering and thirsting after righteousness. He attained satisfaction. From that hour he became a suitable agent in the Divine Hand for the reawakening of the entire Protestant Christendom. Equally instructive is the history of his compeers, Charles Wesley, Whitefield, Fletcher, Nelson, Walsh, and the long list of the early Methodist preachers. These are our ensamples. The insistence on conversion must never be abated. It was our first cry, and must be heard to the end. It is of the essence of the future mission of Methodism to keep bright before the world and before the now helpful Churches this testimony: "Except a man be born of water and of the Spirit, he cannot enter into the kingdom of God."

I may well shrink from speaking to my fathers and elder brethren in the ministry, but there is no impropriety in my addressing myself to the young preachers. I see the Methodism of the future committed into the hands of the young men of the present. Will they suffer me to say that, while fully admiring the breadth of sympathy and the endeavour to attain to a wider range of thought and teaching, which I know to be prevalent amongst them, my calm and deep conviction is, that if they would attain to the highest degree of usefulness, if they would effectually fulfil the ministry of the Lord Jesus, if they would raise up a holy seed for present and future service in the Church, and answer the first and chiefest end of their calling, this must be their central theme. If I may use a perhaps questionable figure in such a connection, this must be the bull's eye of the target.

It has been beautifully said that Methodism began in Bible study, the quiet search there for the paths of holiness. "My brother and I read the Bible; saw inward and outward holiness therein; followed after it, and incited others so to do." Ah! this is Methodism in embryo. First, the quiet Bible study; then the pursuit of the holiness which it sets forth; then the inciting of others to like pursuit. Then follows the preaching. Yes, this was its expansive stage. Methodism was made by preaching. It must be maintained and extended by it. The Methodist ministers are pre-eminently Methodist preachers. No commission approaches the one given by the Lord of All, "Go, preach the gospel." What a sublime study for the young preacher is presented in that one message, "THE GOSPEL"! This is the power of God unto the salvation of them that believe. How sacred a duty is it to learn what the gospel is! And then to go forth with that gospel as a life-giving message, and so to teach men as to compel them to see that they have need to be converted; so to urge home the absolute necessity of repentance from all dead works; so to present the cross of Christ, that men may have no doubt of their personal, individual interest in it; so to preach the gospel, that many may believe; to be restless and unsatisfied if this end be not reached. Not to be content with men being mere "inquirers," but resting not until they can sing in the full assurance of faith :—

> "Now I have found the ground wherein
> Sure my soul's anchor may remain,
> The wounds of Jesus, for my sin
> Before the world's foundation slain;
> Whose mercy shall unshaken stay,
> When heaven and earth are fled away."

Nor must any abatement be made from the clear teaching of the past on the witness of the Divine Spirit to the believer's acceptance. It will be incumbent on them to whom the Methodism of the future is intrusted, carefully to study, and confidently to proclaim, this as the believer's high privilege.

If John Wesley did not leave extensive writings on scientific theology, he left the clearest teachings on the practical aspects of the Christian faith. The sons that bear his name will do themselves no credit by neglecting the study of those writings, with their sentences sharply cut as the facets of a brilliant. The clearly marked lines of practical utility within which the toil of his life was spent, saved him from speculative digressions; while the constant appeal to the divine Scriptures, the supreme authority of which he never questioned, saved him from the fancies of error. What he lacked in novelty he gained in verity; and the future students of his writings will be the best exponents of his system. The young ministers anxious for breadth of view will have no occasion to fear any limitation of their vision from Wesley's writings; and they who are desirous of maintaining a firm fidelity to the authoritative Scriptures will find Wesley to lead them ever back to that fountain.

These remarks apply equally to the doctrine of entire sanctification, or Christian perfection (which may, if any may, be called a Methodist doctrine). Many travesties of this doctrine have been presented to the world, but they were given in ignorance of Wesley's own teaching.

Though I fear to repeat myself, I am compelled to say that one part of the mission of Methodism in the future is the keeping before the Churches (it is not altogether needless to speak of it to those without) the high standard of moral and spiritual life up to which it is at once the duty and the prerogative of every believer in the gospel to aspire. And there is no necessity to deny the delicate, mystic elements in a faithful insistence on its practical embodiment in the duty of life. There is not much danger in these days, nor will there be, I conjecture, in the future, of the mystic absorption of the spirit in mere contemplative stillness. There is a special spiritual culture to be gained in elevated thought, in wrapt reflection, in the withdrawment from the world into a wilderness of quietude in communion with God, in a feasting of the soul on the lofty poetic sentiments of hope and love. To be alone with Christ, away from the world of noise and show, is not to be lost in the reveries of dreamland, though encompassed with "the sacred awe that dares not move." All on this more mystical side of the spiritual life is a permissible indulgence, and may be the truest help to the faithful and fearless practice of all godliness. Whatsoever things are true, just, pure, lovely; yea, every reverend and gracious thing, may be thought upon until thought stirs affection, and affection unfolds itself in the charity that prompts to a ceaseless well-doing to others.

Christian perfection is not Christian nonsense. It is loving God with all the heart, and one's neighbour as one's self; than which there is not a higher, or simpler, or more rational rule of life.

I am here reminded of words which are brought before our attention year by year in that invaluable Methodist preacher's *vade mecum*, " The Pastoral Resolutions : "[1] " Let us preach constantly the leading and vital doctrines of the gospel : repentance toward God; a present, free and full salvation from sin ; a salvation flowing from the grace of God alone, 'through the redemption that is in Christ Jesus,' and apprehended by the simple exercise of faith ; a salvation which begins with the forgiveness of sins, this forgiveness being certified to the penitent believer by the Holy Spirit, and by the power of that Divine Spirit Who bears the witness, a change of heart; a salvation which is the only entrance to a course of practical holiness."

We must not remit these doctrines to the past. How needful is it to-day to try to preach penetrative and effective sermons every Sabbath, not leaving the hope of ingathering to occasional and spasmodic efforts !

I am tempted here to add another sentence from the same " Resolutions," being persuaded that I can say nothing better or half so well. " Remembering that the prominence which is properly given in the Methodist pulpit to the doctrine of a present salvation is ever liable to Antinomian abuses, let us diligently and evangelically

---

[1] I take the opportunity of urging a thoughtful attention to this little Manual. By steadily ordering his steps according to it, every Methodist preacher may successfully fulfil his mission ; beyond the requirements of it no man need be urged, but up to it every one should strive to come.

preach the precepts as well as the privileges of the gospel, expounding them carefully, and applying them faithfully."

I have endeavoured to show how important a place Christian fellowship holds in the constitution of Methodism. I have classed it with the essentials of that constitution. It is pre-eminently a distinguishing characteristic. The importance of this to future Methodism is vital. It would cease to be Methodism without it. Some things it may dispense with; they are adventitious, and not of its essential idea. It could remain Methodism without the men sitting on one side of the chapel and the women on the other. But this cannot be spared. "The spiritual fellowship of Methodism is necessary in order to the life of its evangelical doctrine. Its characteristic doctrine is not only evangelical, but yet more strikingly and specifically is it experimental. Experience—vivid and inspiring experience—is essential to the character and life of Methodism."[1] It is essential to the perfectness of any Church;[2] but Methodism would be no longer Methodism were its fellowship to be eliminated.

It is therefore an obligation of the highest and most sacred character to maintain this principle intact and unimpaired. It is not boasting to affirm that we are the special representatives amongst the Churches of the

---

[1] *A Comparative View of Church Organizations*, by James H. Rigg, D.D.

[2] "Unless a Christian Church, in some effective manner, makes provision for real individual fellowship, fellowship which joins into one living brotherhood the general society of believers, so that each believer may have actual spiritual comradeship with some company of others, and be linked to the whole body in vital and organic connection, and so that all may have an opportunity of using their spiritual faculties and gifts, that Church is essentially defective."—(*Ibid.* p. 11.)

vital importance of a true Christian fellowship. We may have much to learn and much to unlearn as to modes, and as to the distinction between the principle and some traditional forms of manifestation and working; but unswerving fidelity to the essential character of Christian communion will lead us away from crudities of method.

One reason why all attempts hitherto made to give a wider comprehension to our Church have proved unsuccessful, is because it is impossible to take out of Methodism the conviction that it is the duty of every believer to use his talent, his gift, for the good of the whole Church; his privilege to receive personal and constant oversight from the Church; and alike the duty and privilege of all to maintain an actual intercommunion of spiritual sentiment and a real mutual ministry.

Whether Methodism will succeed in persuading the Churches to adopt a method of fellowship similar to that of the class-meeting or not, it will still be its duty to hold up to the Churches an example they would do well to imitate.

I speak at a favourable moment of the capability of Methodism to adapt its agencies to the changed conditions of our large towns, as testified by the success of our new missions. Nor is the time inopportune in which to speak of the imperative demand for Connexional Methodism in our villages. We have proved by experience that our system is able to bring its whole force to bear upon isolated spots with a view to resist local oppression, or to aid in opposing forces which would be omnipotent against separated and unsupported Churches.

Methodism has a special fitness to reach the masses of

the irreligious portion of the population and to deal with them. Are not our simple services adapted to the unenlightened and careless? Is not our Christian fellowship suited to them who have little of home happiness, of comfort, and of friendship? I believe that the kindness, which in the lips of an apostle would be brotherly love, is one of the great glories of the Christian religion, and it has been one of the honours of Methodism to promote it.

It is most obvious that in settling down into a Church, or even in its care for the Society, Methodism would require and would develop the abilities of men varying very greatly in temperament, in attainment, and ability. It could find a place for David Stoner and John Nelson and William Bramwell, also for Richard Watson, for Dr. Coke and Adam Clarke, for Joseph Benson and Jabez Bunting; and so must it be in the future. It will demand the pastor and the teacher, as well as the prophet and the evangelist. It will find work for all such in building up in knowledge and doctrine those who by the evangelistic effort are won over from sin.

Happily the teaching and preaching power has been well cultivated amongst us, and it is not presumptuous to say that we have always hitherto had a large proportion of able and effective preachers. And so long as Methodism has in it a pure spring of spiritual life, so long as men are converted to God by its labours, so long as it is true to Holy Scripture in doctrine and life and godly discipline, so long will it continue to have abundance of spiritual labourers, both clerical and lay. But, passing this by, I feel wishful to emphasize my assertion that we must preserve, as heretofore has been preserved, a class of men whose work is pioneer work—the work of the active, earnest, fervid appellant to the ungodly, the evangelist, the preacher whose word is as a hammer to break in pieces the hardened heart. We must have men adapted by human aptitude and by the divine grace for the especial work of calling sinners to repentance.

In using the term evangelist in this connection, I wish it not to be supposed that I confine the idea of evangelistic work to those whose appeal is made mainly to the wicked and negligent. All service which tends to promulgate the one evangel, to unfold its deeper meaning and its wider application; to promote its influence upon the life and morals of mankind, and even to screen them who accept it from the temptation that would allure them to abandon it, is embraced and properly described by the one word evangelistic.

This is, of course, the work of every Methodist preacher, and the work which every one covets the power, but no effort enables some to do it as do others. They have other gifts, and their work is less obvious. The goodness and serviceableness of their labour can be seen only after many days. On them depends the patient culture and perfecting of the Church. This work may win for them less applause, as it secures for them less affection (for who does not love the father better than the tutor ?). One cannot despise the other, saying, "I have no need of thee." The teacher without the evangelist would have a gradually diminishing number of scholars; the evangelist without the teacher would leave his work a "rope of sand." In many of the more brilliant examples of the Methodist ministry in the past these apparently different qualities have been surprisingly and beneficially combined. But while men covet earnestly the best gifts, this high endowment must not be overlooked. If Methodism in the future is to do work which shall compare with the past, or be in any true sense a fulfilment of it, it must ever be characterized as a *fervent evangelism*. Its primary elements constitute it a *revival*. It is most needful to maintain this characteristic. It has been and must continue to be a determined assault upon sin. Everything must bend to this. The sacred ingenuity which is observable in devising methods to meet new conditions is to be guided and controlled by this aim. It will be but Methodism in name if it be not an evangelism. This is an essential element. It would be contrary to the genius of Methodism were it to settle down into a number of independent Churches, or were its ministers to become located ministers, each caring only for his own flock.

Probably it is not adapted to this latter condition. This is not to its discredit—far from it. All its institutions must be co-ordinated with its essential principles. There are many things which other Churches may do, or which Methodism might do if it were differently constituted; but it has its own service to render amongst the Churches. To copy others would interfere with and probably make vain this its great essential work. Methodism has no need to retire from the very forefront of evangelistic efforts. In the ranks of its ministry are hundreds of men fired with the true spirit; while an army of helpers is presented from its active laity, who are equally willing to devote time and wealth and labour to this good work. Our numerous special missions in London and the provinces both prove the accuracy of this statement and set the example of it. We have need to make a continuous onslaught upon the kingdom of evil in all our Circuits,—an attempt not merely to fill our chapels, and certainly not by any questionable methods, but to bear effectually upon all unrighteousness. Let every Circuit inquire in what way its energies can be brought to bear upon the ungodly around. By this means activities will be aroused that will redeem many a life from stagnation and threatening death.

But I do not suggest a merely temporary and spasmodic effort. I urge no employment of new measures, but the steady, settled pursuit of the one object in the use of the old means; the consecration of the Church's effort in the chapel and the cottage and the open air. I have no vain hope of seeing an entire population changed in a few months. The steady tread of Wesley in paths to which his feet had become accustomed shows the supreme importance of continued and persevering labour.

Grave duties lie before us in the call to improve our public services in reverence and solemnity, in liturgical completeness, and in quietness and order, for the worship of God should be restful to man.

I confess to an insatiable delight in the beauty and touching tenderness of a well-ordered Christian liturgical service; to a fondness for Gothic styles of architecture, for tones of lute and organ, for the utmost proprieties of public worship; but I would sacrifice one and all, if it were necessary, to promote that great work which our forefathers accomplished in barns and wayside cottages, in the square, unsightly meeting-house, or on hillside and in dale,—the conversion of the vile and the outcast, the stirring up of the Church by holy rivalry, not in imitated services and methods, but in a success which is all the more easily wrought amongst the evil and negligent and low, and which is far more charitable.

I have always striven to build up believers by teaching, and to gather and keep the young near to us by those means which are now happily at our command; but I confess, had I my time to come over again, if that time must be given to one thing rather than another, it should be given to that work which our first fathers did; and when the evil ones had been converted and the filthy ones washed, and their habits changed and their circumstances improved, I would rejoice that there were many who could train and culture what I could only rescue.

I delight in the ideal Church. I truly believe Methodism to be a Church, not because we call it one, but because the divine elements within it make it one; but I am prepared to cling (and I do indeed cling) to the old Society structure, if thereby we can do more effectually our own peculiar work. I long for a Methodism to be preserved in the future that shall most strictly answer to John Wesley's own conception of it when he and his companions went forth on their God-sent errand.

I rejoice in Methodism as it is—as it was when I first knew it fifty years ago; but much more as I know it to-day, with its wider influence, its multiplied agencies, its grander future, its revived and specialized home missions, and its undiminished and yet to be extended interest in our colonial and heathen missions. And I only desire a faithful and ardent clinging to the old purpose, the old methods, and the old spirit.

It is difficult to imagine anything that is not within the

boundaries of the work which the Churches of the present day set themselves more or less earnestly to do. The preaching of the word, always regarded in Protestant communities as the Church's pre-eminent work, is in some danger of being thrown into the background by the many subsidiary works of a benevolent, educational, or social character that have come to be regarded as part of the Church's duty. Time is absorbed and attention demanded by social and mental improvement, artistic and scientific societies, clothing and reading clubs, even public amusements, athletic clubs for young men, and evening concerts for wearied artisans; while all the Churches are deeply interested in the many endeavours to promote sobriety and arrest the incalculable evils of drunkenness, as is testified by the large Temperance Societies, Bands of Hope for the young, and the watchfulness over the legislation affecting these questions. The Churches have been led not only to ally themselves with the recreations and intellectual pursuits, but to take the lead in promoting and controlling them, driven to this by the danger of the indiscriminate association of the young, and as a counter-attraction to allure them from questionable entertainments. Possibly a little denominational rivalry stimulates to this ingenuity and inventiveness. It is a Christian citizen's duty to fulfil his part in promoting the enactment of wise and beneficent laws; and Christian ministers cannot in the present day ignore the duties of citizenship.

Great social problems are demanding solution. The messengers of Christ, Who cared for the bodies as well as the souls of men, see it to be their duty to promote the well-housing of the poor, and the improvement of the public health by correct sanitary laws. Lessons of thrift, of foresight and frugality, are proper for the lips of them who aim at the entire redemption of the human life. Nor is it beyond the range of a prudent ministerial activity, as we have recently seen, to endeavour to aid in the adjustment of the strained relations of different classes of society. And concurrently with this the use of the mighty engine for social renovation, the press, lays its claim upon the energies of the Churches. The condition of our poor, and their sad tendency to gravitate to lower and lower depths of misery and want, claim the most thoughtful attention. An expansive spirit of philanthropy distinguishes the present times, and it cannot be said to be inimical to the benevolent character of Christianity to care for the human life in all its needs, or to promote social ameliorations wherever it is possible to do so.

One effect of this is to bind up the whole life in some sort of alliance with the Church, to bring all its interests under the shadow of the Church's wings, and to secure for all human activities the Church's blessing. And as the spirit of Christianity permeates the national mind, we see approaching the true identity of the interests of the Church and the State. And we have little fear in these days that the Church as a mere organization will in any sense override and dominate the State as in days gone by. But if, concurrently with all this necessary work, fidelity to the divine commission be maintained, the Church's pure truth be taught, and the gospel's pure spirit be breathed, the truest ends of the Church's existence will be answered, the secret springs of human activity will be touched, and its energies evoked by an inspiration of the national life with principles of righteousness, peace, and goodwill.

It will be the duty of Methodism to continue to take its share in all this ameliorative work, and the more so because it has so close an affinity with the working population of the country. Whatever Methodism is adapted to do at any period of its history, that is its mission and calling to do. It has no specialized mission to the wealthier and more educated classes of English society. It has its one gospel for all, rich and poor alike; none are so poor as the rich are without the gospel; but there is nothing in its services or its teaching or modes of working to make it specially fitted to the higher grades of English life. That men and women rise in the social scale from the homes of Methodism is easily to be understood and accounted for; and that the principles of Methodism may be brought into contact with these classes to their great and lasting benefit, we know. But our peculiar methods have never had any attraction for them or special adaptation to them. It will be one of the duties of Methodism in the future to adapt itself more and more to all conditions.

Nor does it arrogate to itself a capability of meeting all the necessities of English life. It has proved itself adapted to the conditions of American and colonial life, and to the requirements of newly formed nations.

Methodism is not indifferent to the general uplifting of the national life, or to those ameliorations of the suffering and ignorant which have ever called forth the toil and the sacrifice of philanthropic individuals and communities. Who could be a true follower of Wesley and remain indifferent to these things! One of the many pleasing and not the least interesting points of view from which Wesley may be regarded, is that which enables us to see this cultivated life giving itself to unequalled labours in the endeavour to uplift English society, not only by the preaching of a gospel which could renovate the character, but by the publication of grammars and histories, of works on natural science, of tracts and of treatises, by the provision of good, wholesome literature at a low cost for the cottage-labourer and the poor, opening schools for the ignorant and orphanages for the outcast, infirmaries for the sick, and other institutions for the relief of poverty and suffering and ignorance, and by his many works of an educational, benevolent, and ameliorative character.

But while we give his meed of praise to the man who did so much in an age when others did so little, we must not forget that the traditions of good work done in the past do not relieve the present or the future from its high obligations. If Methodism is to retain its hold in coming time on that large section of the people amongst whom its chief labour has been expended, it must continue to manifest an ever-increasing interest in those great social questions which affect the welfare of that class in particular.

Methodism has not lagged behind the Churches hitherto in philanthropic endeavours. If it has not had the means at command for doing great works, it has, according to its opportunity and within the scope of its ability, been faithful in this class of service. Witness its care for the young in its Sunday schools, so early begun and so widely expanded; its day-school education, so honourably pursued when the nation was neglecting its duty. Let not the future be shamed by the past.

I cannot be silent on the subject of Foreign Missions— the grandest, the most charitable, the most Christlike work the Church ever attempted. Is Methodism going to be unfaithful to its trust in this matter? Will its zeal abate; its charity grow cold? Will its care for the heathen wither and die? Will it sink into a cold self-absorption? I cannot believe it. Were it to do so, the very stones would cry out. Methodism indifferent to Christian missions! What a traitorous spirit must it harbour before this could be! What an offence against all our traditions! What a crime before the world! What a repulse to the young men who are offering themselves for the work, and would do so in multiplied numbers if assurance were given that the offers would not be in vain! I know assuredly what is the sentiment of home students respecting the foreign work.

We read of candlesticks being removed out of their places. Could anything more loudly call for the divine displeasure than that the Church, which above all Churches has been honoured in its missions, should become deaf to a call of duty it has hitherto delighted to hear?

Our forefathers in this land sacrificed their sons and their daughters on the flaming pile to the sun and moon. Is heathenish blindness to put to shame enlightened Christian parents, who will not give their sons as sacrifices for the redemption of the nations, or give of their wealth to this godlike enterprise? No, no. It cannot be. So long as the grace of God attends our ministry, so long will our converts be ready to offer life and substance on this altar.

Methodism (in my use of the term) embraces not only the Wesleyan Methodist Connexion, but also the surrounding Methodist Churches which under various circumstances have been separated from it, flung off like satellites, by some strong disintegrating centrifugal power, it may be, but to be reabsorbed, we may hope, by a greater centripetal force.

What is the adaptation of Methodism in its totality to help towards meeting the world's great want? I am far from supposing that even the aggregate Churches bearing this name are capable of overtaking that want. All the exertions of all the Churches combined must be consecrated to this great work. Of course this entire cluster of Churches has its aim in common with all the Churches—the universal diffusion of the gospel. It cannot be satisfied with less than this. Hailing and rejoicing in every effort made to accomplish this end, by whomsoever made, it is restless until it is attained.

My strong conviction is that the duty of the several communities who claim Wesley as their real Founder, is to take every opportunity of making known their essential unity and of encouraging a well-devised and prudent effort to promote actual unity. Is there any living Church to-day on whom it is more incumbent to engage in a great world-wide effort for the general uplifting of mankind—to raise a united cry against widespread social and national evils, to promote righteousness in national life and legislation, to insist on the highest moral principles in international intercourse? Combined, Methodism may be a great power amongst the nations.

Some have discerned a possible calling of Methodism to

be to act the part of mediator, a connecting link between the Churches. Its relation to the Church of England on the one hand and to the nonconforming Churches on the other; the acknowledged indebtedness of both to its service and influence; its freedom from political bias; its firm adhesion to the past, and its openness to the teachings of the present, all help to qualify it to bridge the distance between widely separated communities, and to be "the friend of all, the enemy of none." If we are to retain our isolation from one another, any such service must be indefinitely postponed.

Does it not behove us to vindicate our position to ourselves and to the Churches, if not to the world without, the progress of whose welfare we may hinder by our separation from one another?

The mission of Methodism is not sectarian. We ought to resolve to cleave to the Churches generally with as much determination as Wesley to the last sought to cleave to the Church of England; but what ought to be the mutual attitude of Churches whose doctrinal beliefs, forms of worship, and essential peculiarities declare an inner unity which it is a disgrace to our common name to contradict by our outward separation?

There is a miserable partition between the Methodist Churches of this land, which I trust I may live to see destroyed. It sprang as we know from many causes; but one cause—the unapproachable preciousness of the interests of Christ's Church and of immortal souls—ought to make it soon to be a thing of the past. When shall we rise above the petty prejudices which drive the inhabitants of a village to worship in two, three, or even four little chapels, when any one of them would hold all the worshippers together?

But there is a true, deep, underlying unity of all the Churches owning Wesley as their Founder, and an external union which is growing in power and in obvious evidences. It was declared by the Œcumenical Conference in City Road Chapel, and will be by the forthcoming Œcumenical Conference in America. In that Conference Methodism will, I trust, rise to a discernment of its true, its immeasurably great and honourable calling of God, in a oneness of spirit, of aim, and of enterprise. In speaking of the mission of Methodism, I cannot pass by this important subject. If I have any advantage in speaking from this position, and can use my position to give the slightest impulse to so good and desirable a work as the real, hearty unification of Methodism, I shall be profoundly thankful, and I will count it an ample repayment for the toil of preparing myself to occupy it.

Is it that we have not grace enough to enable us to be at one in brotherly fellowship; or is it that we have not wit enough to know how to bring it about? Are we checked by its difficulty, or hindered by a supposed imprudence in the first effort to effect it? Is any one of these the cause of our continued divisions, or are all together? Or is the bitterness of painful recollections, or the vanity of supposed superiority, or the jealousy of numerical inferiority, or the manœuvring of political partisanship, or the supineness of sinful indifference to be charged with it? Is any one of these a worthy cause, or an insurmountable barrier? Can they not be overcome? Does not the common name that we bear call us to strive by all means within our power to overcome them, that we may show to the world that we can sink the littleness of our diversities in the greatness of our common aim?

Why should there not be a *combined* effort to fulfil the mission of Methodism, an effort of mutual help and mutual arrangement? There must be concession in the interests of unity. The spirit of Christ calls for it; the spirit of reviling without demands it; the necessities of the age cry aloud for it! The call to unity of *action* is imperative.

Every form of Methodism on this side of the water should be so united as to present the front of a common Methodism to the world. And were every one of the several great bodies on the other side of the water, in America, in Canada, also in the Colonies, to unite in one great effort to urge forward the world's regeneration, by mutual counsel, mutual help, forbearance, and consideration; by judicious arrangement of plans, by harmony and fellowship in labour, who shall declare its happy effects? "That there are practical difficulties in the way of immediately effecting a union, does not in the least invalidate the assertion that disunion ought not to exist."[1] The whole of Methodism in this country at least ought to form a confederation of Churches true to the great and avowed principles of Methodism, each retaining, if still needful, its own individual freedom, but all bearing one testimony; and not continuing to be split up into factions.

Can we as communities dare to sing the hymns which were written for the little companies of believers? I have thought that our not having sung these hymns with greater

[1] Dr. Rigg, p. 291.

frequency is one reason why we have not approached each other more willingly. O that Methodists, the wide world over, could be baptized into one spirit, could seize upon one aim, could submit to one inspiration! Their work is a divine work, divine in its origin, in its aims. O that it were conformed to the divine ideal!

> "One the Father is with Thee;
> Knit us in like unity.
> Make us, O uniting Son,
> One, as Thou and He are one.
>
> Jesus, Lord, we look to Thee,
> Let us in Thy name agree;
> Show Thyself the Prince of Peace,
> Bid our jars for ever cease."

Nor is the mission of Methodism merely national—it is world-wide. I must again lift up my voice with an earnest entreaty to all Methodism to unite. It was my pleasure to take part in the last Methodist Œcumenical Conference, when a fire that had long smouldered within was fanned to a fervent heat of desire that we might be one. What will the coming Conference do towards promoting this? To elaborate mere details and leave these great questions undecided would be sacrificing the higher for lower interests.

Can we not combine in our missions? Can we not do something more than merely send over friendly visitants? Let us exult in something above the enumeration of chapels, and schools, and scholars — something more, something greater, something beyond. Let us inquire, *What can we combine to do for the world's good?* How truly we may say, how effectually we might prove, "The world is my parish"!

But Methodism need not be alone in this. It is part of its mission to unite all the Churches, and nothing less can be its present duty than a loving coalition, melting down all selfishness, fusing all in one patient, united, undying effort to save the world. I fear the coldness which the Churches show towards one another is one reason why the world turns away in cold suspicion from us all.

Is it useless to long for one united crusade against heathenism and sin? Must the poor Christian Church long continue to struggle on in rival communities before the grand display of combined charity to a dying world is made? I do not design by this any hope of an organic union of the Churches. That dream is vain at present, and will pass away into a reality only when the morning, the bright morning of the millennial day shall awaken the Churches to their true grandeur and duty; but why may there not be an organized effort, a mutual compact, not to interfere with each other, and certainly not to be antagonistic, but in every way to help one another? Were it not a graceful act, and, if accomplished, would it not be an influential act, if we took the initiative in this, standing as we do midway between the Church of which we were born and the Salvation Army, which was born of us, and being in close proximity to the Churches which are the descendants of the Puritan era?

Again, in presence of the world's carelessness, and its readiness to find excuses for despisal of the Churches, in presence of many fierce onslaughts on the Church's faith, and world-wide demands on the Church's charity, I plead for every obstacle 'to be taken out of the way; and I affirm that one of the greatest of these is to be found in our petty divisions. Was there no discernment of this when the prayer ascended to heaven—"That they all may be one, that the world may believe that Thou hast sent me"?

What a humiliating circumstance it is that in these days we have to draw the attention of men to the gospel by drums, and fifes, and fiddles, by duets and solos! Is it that the gospel is lacking in those great elements which alone can engage the sympathies of mankind—that it lacks grandeur, or beauty, or evidence of truth? Or is it that we have faultily presented the gospel to the world, so that an erroneous estimate of it has been formed by the multitude, and they do not know or believe that it is indeed of God? Or are we to explain it all by the natural revolt from what is spiritual, or that which imposes a restraint upon the passions of the heart of man and the appetites of the flesh? Those tambourines and trumpets may be evidences of the earnestness of effort and ingenuity of device on the part of good men and women. But they are a disgrace to the world that needs them, and will not be drawn to God without them; a disgrace to the Church that is driven to use them, if not indeed a disgrace to the gospel truth, or to the gospel messengers that can by no other means win attention.

If I were asked, What are the distinguishing features of our economy which in any degree fit it for special usefulness in the future?

1. I would first name *the simple terms of our Church membership*. We do not ask from men the proofs of goodness before admitting them to our fellowship. The one requirement is having a desire to be good, "to flee from

the wrath to come, and to save their souls;" no special doctrinal beliefs or freedom from doctrinal errors being demanded. The Church of Christ can scarcely be a home only for the good. Sinful, suffering men need a place of healing, a Bethesda. Christ's mission was to the sick, the blind, the lame, the halt, to men possessed with devils. He was a Physician. The physician labours amongst the sick. What healer seeks out the healthy? He came " not to call the righteous, but sinners to repentance." The true picture is that of the fallen one crouching at the door, filthy, half-clothed and half-starved, asking for admission. But no sooner is the wanderer within the house than all efforts must be made to succour, to wash, to comfort, to clothe, that, in his right mind, he may sit at the feet of Jesus.

How often have we seen this enacted in the class-meeting! Then follows the true fellowship, the companionship, the brotherhood of the Church, where the exposed spirit may be guarded from the fellowship of evil, and the enfeebled by sin be made strong by instruction in righteousness. Something analogous to this every Church should present. This equality and thoroughness of Christian fellowship is an ideal of Methodism. I have treated of it elsewhere. If it has been our calling and endowment to initiate this and to teach the Churches how great is the benefit of it, it will be part of our joy to see the whole Church imitate, or even improve upon, our example.

2. I would refer secondly to our *Itinerating Ministry*. I am ready at once to concede that there are both advantages and disadvantages in it. Some of the latter are obvious. The day is probably at hand when some change

in its severely marked lines may be made. But its advantages are great. In it the enriched stores of many years are expended upon a short period of time, which must be a gain to the congregations. There is no occasion for poverty of teaching when the best products of reading, and observation, and of tested methods of work are spread over so brief a space; while the renewal of devotion, the stimulus of new enterprise and new surrounding, is very great. Unwholesome pools are found where the waters are stagnant. Our free and constant circulation promotes sweetness, and is in harmony with life. Stagnation seems almost impossible where change is so frequent, and even unfitness for a particular sphere to which a minister may be appointed is speedily corrected by removal. More time is put at the disposal of a minister, for there can be no sufficient reason why a prudent use may not be made of previous preparations for the pulpit. It would be impossible for Methodist preachers to do the amount of work that is done by them were it not for the opportunity of thus utilizing past efforts.

A further benefit is found in the interest which every minister is led to feel in the whole of Methodism. The frequent change of Circuit, the occasional interchange with neighbouring ministers, the weekly Circuit meeting, the monthly meeting of the ministers of the same town, the annual District meetings, and the Conference, in which all Methodist affairs are investigated, put every man in touch with the whole. The interchange of pulpits in the Circuit is another considerable advantage, and the inevitable, as well as the constituted, oversight which the group of ministers gives, prevents faults from being hidden. No man can long propagate error or be faulty in conduct without its being known. The weak are strengthened and the timid cheered, and the defects of one teacher are supplied by the others. There is a greater breadth of instruction than could be given were the labours of one man continued through many years to the same people.

I am not unmindful of the drawbacks to all this—the loss of personal influence in a given locality, which could be gained only by prolonged residence ; the sense of unrest which both Circuits and ministers feel; the interruption of schemes that require time for their completion; the lack of continuity in teaching; the frequent breaking up of ties of friendship; the disappointment on the removal of a favourite minister; the inconvenience and family discomfort on the preacher's side; the inevitable overlooking of individuals and even families in the frequent process of change. All these and many others are a serious discount from a system which for purposes of aggressive effort has no equal.

That some modifications might with advantage be made is becoming the conviction of an increasing number. To draw tighter the bonds of relationship between the ministers and the people (though where are closer and more affectionate attachments to be found ?), to secure the benefit of more continuous effort, and to avoid the injury of interrupted plans, to prevent loss by inevitable and painful changes, to save labour and time and even expense incurred, urge to it.

3. But all these fail to counterbalance the good which a Church like Methodism, with its *Connexionalism*, its

united ministry and common interests, and its aggressive character, must gain from a plan which utilizes all that is best in the Church, not for the benefit of a favoured few, but for the good of the many, and which prevents selfish isolation and independence. The itinerant ministry binds Methodism together as with iron bands, and makes it a power for united action which has excited the surprise and admiration of many onlookers.

4. I would further name *the association of the laity to so large an extent with the ministry in the management of all matters relating to the Church*. There is scarcely anything that is not personal to the ministers in the management of which the laity are not identified. I am very far from having confidence in an untutored democracy, but I cannot be indifferent to the strong tendency of the age towards democratic institutions, with which to a large extent Methodism is in harmony. It has always held within itself a wise regard to the claims of all classes. How truly is this seen in the conditions of our Societies! Not only in the larger town Societies, but in every little country Society, each is governed really from within itself. Its officers, leaders, stewards, local preachers are taken from among the members themselves. Each is a little republic; but each enjoys the benefit of the grouping together of a number of adjacent congregations for mutual help and support, which characterizes our Circuit system. Nothing restrains us from adapting our methods to new circumstances as they arise. But we are restrained—we must restrain ourselves—from sacrificing our principles at any time to the deceit of the hour.

5. I may also refer to *our freedom from anything in*

our constitution that would place us in antagonism to other Churches.

The essential mission of Methodism is a spiritual one. This is to be carefully distinguished from its outward form. With the exception of a few simple principles, to which it was called to give prominence—*e.g.* Christian fellowship, the employment of the gifts of every member of the Church, its itinerant and lay preaching, its Connexionalism, and a large measure of lay influence in its Church Courts,—it has no special teaching on Church organization to give. It did not set out with the purpose of giving any, or in any spirit of divergence from existing types. The great body of Dissent places itself in opposition to the theory of an Establishment and to Episcopacy, in which latter it is at one with all Presbyterian Churches, though not at one with them in regard to the theory of the Church. Methodism did not arise in any one of these lines of divergence; nor did it, as a community, assume any attitude of antagonism to these views; although, as we have seen, Wesley did not hold Episcopacy to be the only true form of Church government. It does not now exist merely as a protest against any other form of Church organization, although it bears its silent tribute to some, and its equal testimony against the assumptions of others. We deny not the validity of Episcopal Church orders, solely the validity of their exclusiveness. But if it is Presbyterian as opposed to Episcopalianism, it is not a political dissent as against the principle of Church Establishments. Individual members are at liberty to hold and teach their views on these subjects, but Methodism as a system can proceed in utter ignorance of them. Other nonconformist Churches of the land exist mainly as protests against assumption, or against what is held to be error in doctrine or Church organization, or some other feature supposed to contradict the scriptural ideal. Whatever may be the actual relation of Methodism to these questions, it did not originate, nor does it exist, simply as a revolt from them. Its *raison d'être* does not lie in its ecclesiastical structure, however well adapted that may be to its high purpose, but in its spiritual calling and capabilities.

It has been said that as a system of Church organization it is complicated and highly organized. This is a description, not an accusation. Perhaps this arises partly from the fact that its nomenclature gives an air of novelty to it, partly from the fact that every detail comes regularly under review. It is a machine whose parts are well articulated, every tooth in every wheel of which is seen, and at stated times is carefully examined. Nothing is hidden; every joining bolt and screw is statedly tapped and tested.

I am far from claiming for Methodism any exclusive fitness to be the Church of the future. But I do not hesitate to affirm my deliberate judgment that no Church will gain a permanent hold upon human society, or will meet its far-reaching spiritual needs, that does not contain within itself those principles which are the essential characteristics of Methodism.

It appears to me that the Church which would prove itself to be best fitted to meet the needs, and secure the adhesion, and guide the destinies of the coming times, must be prepared to hold fast to the essential doctrines and principles of Holy Scripture, and yet leave free play for the adjustment of details and theories, according to the progressive knowledge of the race, the light that waxes towards the perfect day, the growth which renders less and less necessary the restriction which our Lord declared once to exist, " Ye cannot bear them now." It must not be afraid of science justly so-called, whether it be science of history or of language, of mind or of external and physical nature ; but, receiving all truth as light given from on high to make clearer the unfathomable depths of the holy mysteries, it must not bind the teaching of to-day within rigid lines.

At the same time it must neither be flippant in its treatment of the convictions of the past, nor doubtful or distrustful or independent of the spiritual and divine forces which all the great reformers of the past declared to be not merely the chief, but the only true sources of their might. Spiritual in character, in order to be an effective agent in a spiritual kingdom, it must be submissive to a spiritual, a divine, instruction, guidance and control, and more and more reliant upon the divine elements of its message, and the divine agencies by which alone even a faithful setting forth of that message can be made effective. The Church that can lead the world most readily into the paths of righteousness, and can most carefully guard the moral interests of men from evil—judging most sternly every harlot that corrupts the earth with her fornication ; the Church that proves itself to be most tenderly considerate for the poor and the sick, and most anxious for the progress and general welfare of all ; that seizes most effectually upon the mind and purpose of Christ, and most meekly exhibits them in action ; that can best manifest His spirit and show most of His charity and truth, His patience towards opposers,

His purity and disinterestedness; the Church that is calmly and seriously earnest in Christian work and lofty in Christian character; that, allowing no truckling with moral obligation (which the world in its instructed conscience will never tolerate), can find the most attractive home for the sinner and give him the strongest assurance of a conquest over his sins; that is best adapted to raise the moral tone of the life of the world; that can best harmonize the relations of different classes of men and lead them to the love of God and the love of one another, binding the scattered ones in flocks as with a shepherd's care;—in a word, the Church that can most nearly approximate itself to the spirit and service of Christ will be the Church to which the awakened world will give its adhesion, without waiting to inquire for any other signs of apostleship, believing that they are most truly sent by the Master who bring most of the Master's spirit in their bosom, and that the real life is in them who are truly dead to all other life beside.

To that Church men will look which can say, without its words proving empty and vain, "Come unto Christ, ye that labour and are laden, and I will lead you to rest;" and to which the world can bring its sick and mourning and outcasts for relief and comfort and kinship. For the world will expect the Church, if it is to prove its divine origin and calling, to be helpful in healing all the wounds of humanity.

That Church will be the chief and the greatest in the eyes of coming generations that can show itself most nearly to approach the condition of being least in its own eyes; that is removed the farthest from boasting and exclusiveness; that can declare by holy deed, and not by noisy assertion, "I am among you as he that serveth."

For a time Churches may be attractive from external conditions. Wealth, position, numbers, social status, or even novelty of methods, and other similar attractions, may draw men for a time; but as assuredly as the Church's Lord coveted none of these things, and paid no court to them, so assuredly the Church which can show its freedom from them, and which can manifest the nearest approach to "The Son of man hath not where to lay His head," will in the long run prove itself to be the Church for the peoples.

The Church will never grow by cherishing a worldly spirit, or prevail by entertaining earthly aims, or conquer by the use of carnal weapons. The Captain of this host "makes war" only "in righteousness." And the awakened world will care nothing for a Church that does not reveal righteousness, a divine righteousness in human dress. The Son of God may be a true Son of man, for a time misunderstood; but the world is too well instructed not to be able to discern Him when He is really present. The divine elements must be there, and the human elements must be there also. The Church must not be above, afar off, separated, alone. Every act of self-seeking and self-glorification, all undue assumption of superiority, is a fetter upon the free action and a weakening of the true strength of the Church, whose Master girded Himself with a towel, and, kneeling down, washed the feet of His disciples. If men in red shirts and women in black bonnets show more of the spirit of Christ than do others, though the onlookers may be repulsed by ignorance or irreverence, they will in time draw near to listen and bear home a charitable, if silent, approval, and pay true homage in the heart to the Master Who gave such gifts to His servants. And we may exhibit the cross of Christ in pure gold outside our churches, but if the spirit of Christ be not within, the world will pass by and not enter the doors. How plainly is this parable expounded in the many cities of the Continent of Europe at this hour!

The age, in as far as it is removed from the contagion of evil, is in earnest search for the right, the true, and the pure. It will not be content to find these in art and miss them in religion. Pleased with beauty of form, it will not be satisfied without beauty in the conduct of life. In a gospel professing to be divine, it will expect the evidences of a divine power. If it was wrong to challenge the Master, it is not wrong to demand of the servant, "What sign showest thou?" And in as far as this age stands opposed to Christianity, it can be conquered only by the power of God, the power of the Spirit.

Whether any one Church will more than others exhibit these qualities, it is needless now to inquire; but it is only in proportion as they are exhibited that any of the Churches will gain the confidence of the outside world, and, as a true agent of the one Great Master, draw all men unto Him.

If I may say in a word what I look upon as our great work, I would say, The mission of Methodism in the future is the faithful adhesion to its own principles,—

1stly, *In giving prominence to the spirituality of religion;*

2ndly, *In maintaining strict fidelity to scriptural doctrine;*

3rdly, *In persevering illustration of the true fellowship of believers;*

4thly, *In the upholding and expansion of home and foreign evangelism;*

5thly, *In ceaseless efforts to promote social advancement.*

It must, in fellowship with all the Churches, aim at the subjection of the national life to the dominion of heartfelt and high-toned religion—the one means which can safely guide the nation through the throes of coming political and social struggles, and save it from effects which it would be fearful to contemplate, if the great power now being intrusted to large bodies of irresponsible men were uncontrolled by the highest moral principle.

I should fail in the completeness of my work if I did not indicate one or two sources of danger which, like slight clouds, streak an otherwise bright sky, and which it is needful we should carefully guard against, lest they imperil the successful fulfilment of our mission. Of course we must be exposed to the peril common to all the Churches, in the unsettling of the faith of our people which is caused by the untoward criticism of the Christian claims (so much of it rude or irreverent) which distinguishes this hour. But a much more subtle danger to our character as a Christian community lurks in the tendency to worldliness which in many forms threatens to eat into the vigour and delicacy of the spiritual life of our people. The Conference has on several occasions called attention to both these dangers in its pastoral addresses to the Societies.[1] It is not every one who duly appreciates the injury to spirituality which comes from questionable amusements and frivolous and self-indulgent pursuits. As the state of the general health affects the power of vision, so moral vigour is needful

[1] See especially *Min. Conf.* 1888, pp. 331-333.

if we would see clearly the kingdom of heaven in its relation to the fascinating occupations of times of relaxation.

I have no sympathy with narrowness at any time, and certainly not with breadth, when that word is used as a synonym for laxity and unchastened licence of expression; and every vagary of human thought is not worthy to be entitled breadth of view. Sure I am that with all the noble generosity of sentiment which usually characterizes the discussions and decisions of our Conference, it is imperative that we be not lax in respect of our doctrinal teaching or our interpretation of our doctrinal standards. I have sometimes feared lest men should be tempted to fail in duteous attention to the working out of our Methodist principles and usages; but this can apply but to a very few. Am I wrong in referring to the injurious tendency sometimes manifested to make great and sudden changes in our policy and methods of working, to which our unrestricted free speech exposes us; or to the danger of placing too great dependence upon novelties, or mere re-arrangements of our methods; or to the possible injury to our preaching from the "free and easy" style that sometimes characterizes what are called "popular addresses"?

I do not say these things in any carping or complaining spirit. I know and love my brethren too well to be betrayed into such a temper; and I believe that so long as we are faithful to the great questions of conversion and the sanctification of life, and while in brotherly fidelity we avoid jealousy, suspicion, and distrust of each other, the Lord in the midst of us will defend and lead us as of old.

I am jealous for Methodism, not because of its interesting

history, though I delight in that history; nor because of its great names, though many of them are to me as ointment poured forth; but because I see that God has given us great advantages for carrying on His gracious purpose of saving the world and lifting men up to righteousness.

I am not jealous concerning any particular form of Church government and organization. Episcopalianism, Presbyterianism, Congregationalism, Connexionalism have each its own excellences, and, as Wesley said, "There must, in the nature of things, be numberless accidental varieties in the government of various Churches."[1] Yet I cannot profess to be careless or indifferent respecting the details of the Church's organization; but any organization, however elaborate, or however simple, will be a dead weight upon the world if it be not vitalized by the spirit of Christ. To give heed to the outward and visible, and be negligent of the inward and spiritual power, would be worse than useless But that system which can most effectually call into play the entire energies of the Church; which can associate representatives of all classes in its administration while retaining an effective government; which can make it to be the acknowledged prerogative of each member of the body to have a personal interest in everything pertaining to the body, and can impress upon each his personal duty and responsibility in respect of everything relating to it, will possess elements that must of necessity characterize the Church that the future will need, if not indeed the only Church the future will tolerate. But it must be suffused with the true spirit. Spirit will yet reign in this age, which is already ceasing to be a materialistic age.

[1] *Min. Conf.* 1747.

Why should not Methodism do a surpassingly great work in the future? We are fettered by no rigid system of Church mechanism, nor by any dogmas that could possibly cramp our energies, or restrain our inquiry, or limit our usefulness. Our few distinguishing doctrines are like clear pebbles from the brook. O for the self-control in the habits of life which gives precision to the eye and steadiness to the hand and strength to the right arm! O for a single aim and a sure trust in our simple weapon! There have never been greater conquests than those achieved by the very sling which we hold in our right hand to-day. O for a faith in God and a true, abiding persuasion that "THE BATTLE IS THE LORD'S"! The old gospel, the world's gospel, wielded as our fathers wielded it, is still God's power for salvation.

I must emphasize here an old, an ever-present truth; namely, that the interests of a spiritual kingdom can be advanced only by spiritual agencies. The men who speak to the world to-day must be like the men of old who "spake from God, being moved by the Holy Ghost."[1]

I cannot restrain the expression of an eager desire that Methodism may completely meet the demands which the future will make upon it. It cannot, any more than can other Churches, rest in the achievements and the traditions of the past, how brilliant soever they may be. Without continuous fidelity to its high commission and trust, it would lose its power and float down the ages disowned of God and despised of men.

Brethren, what a depth, a solemnity, a sacredness of meaning is hidden in that one word *fidelity!* What possi-

[1] 2 Pet. i. 21.

bilities God has given to us! How great a trust has He reposed in us! How terrible a loss for the world would our unfaithfulness be! My last word must be to them whose it will be in the future either to maintain the honour of "that form of Christianity which is called Methodism," or to allow that honour to be trailed in the dust. What a shame it would be if, after all this great work has been done by your fathers, you, into whose hands this beautiful work is committed, should prove unfaithful to your trust! O brethren, Methodism needs little mending at your hands, but it does need your fidelity—fidelity to its principles, its aims, its methods, and its spirit! With faithfulness to a calling which has proved itself to be of God; faithful to the word of truth, insisting on the old cry, "Ye must be born again;" faithful in the pursuit and practice of all holiness; faithful in promoting Christian fellowship, and in ceaseless, world-wide evangelism, in sacrificial toil and unselfish service; faithful to all the traditions of the past, in reliance upon the Divine Spirit, the one Spirit that stands in opposition to all the power of evil; faithful to God, Who giveth so liberally, and to the great world that needeth so keenly, Methodism in your hands may be a joy and a praise in the earth, a spring of blessing to all, and may fulfil in the future the anticipations of its founder, when he said: "We have strong reason to hope that the work He hath begun He will carry on until the day of the Lord Jesus; that He will never intermit this blessed work of His Spirit until He has fulfilled all His promises, until He hath put a period to sin and misery and infirmity and death, and re-established universal holiness and happiness, and caused all the inhabitants of the earth

to sing together, 'Hallelujah, the Lord God omnipotent reigneth. Blessing and glory and wisdom and honour and power and might be unto our God for ever and ever.'"[1]
AMEN.

[1] Sermon on "The General Spread of the Gospel."

APPENDIX.

A. Page 36.

"The mighty charm which gathered crowds and moved their hearts was found in what St. Paul calls the preaching of 'Christ crucified.' The love of God in sending His Son into the world, the self-sacrifice of that Son in life and death, the offering He made for human guilt upon the cross of Calvary, His patience and tenderness, His mediation and intercession,—these were the themes which laid hold on the moral nature of Englishmen by thousands and thousands, and made them what the New Testament calls 'new creatures in Christ Jesus.' It was the substance of the sermons, more than the form and delivery, which produced the effect. Earnest impassioned oratory can never explain what was accomplished. Employed on other themes, it could secure no similar results. Twenty, thirty thousand people crowded together to hear the Methodist preacher: why could not the metaphysician and the moral philosopher do the same with his enchantments, and so, according to his own ideas, help to deliver his fellow-countrymen from what he called the bondage of superstition?"—(Stoughton, vol. vi. p. 428.)

B. Page 54.

"The class-meeting amongst the Methodists is their method of meeting one of the greatest difficulties of the times. It does not profess to impose a new condition of membership in the Christian Church. It is only one out of many forms—certainly the most widespread and permanent—which the Ecclesiola in Ecclesiâ, or the Society within the Church, has assumed. No religious community has long maintained its vigour and purity without some such expedient. This one in particular honours the Church's note of external sanctity by admitting freely every anxious applicant on the sole condition that he, as a baptized member of the Church of Christ, is desirous to flee from the wrath to come, and to find salvation in the name of Jesus. It brings every one under pastoral supervision, direct or indirect: indirect, as the leaders of these classes are themselves part of the minister's flock; and direct, inasmuch as these little companies are under the discipline of a quarterly visitation. This institution provides the means of mutual social edification, in addition to the general means of grace, and thus does much to promote both the external and the internal sanctity of the community: the external, because it tends to give more reality and dignity to the outward fellowship of the Christian Church; the internal, because it brings all the members under the influence of an edifying mutual exhortation and prayer. Apart from its modern name, this form of fellowship may be traced almost up to the times of the apostles."—(*A Compendium of Christian Theology*, William B. Pope, D.D., vol. iii. p. 279.)

C. PAGE 93.

"The things which seemed to be most adverse in this, as in a thousand examples, have turned rather to the furtherance of the gospel. Persecution and hindrance were just what Wesley needed most for the perfecting of his own character, and the new methods on which he was forced were just what the extending dimensions and growing freedom of his work imperatively required. He ceased to be a priest of the Church as by law established, he became the apostle of the eighteenth century."—(Rogers, p. 570.)

D. PAGE 106.

"Any adequate accounts of Wesley would have to include an estimate of his amazing activity as the leader of a great religious organization. He founded a body which, eighty years after his death, could boast of twelve million adherents; and its reaction upon other bodies was perhaps as important as its direct influence."

"His talents for business and for spiritual influence are stamped upon his writings, and command equally our sympathy and our wonder. No such leader of men appeared in that century. . . . . For the immediate purpose of stirring the stagnating currents of religious emotion, no man could have been more admirably endowed."

"His aim is to stamp out vice, to suppress drinking and debauchery, and to show men the plain path to heaven, and force them into it by intelligible threats and promises. He differs, of course, from the ordinary moralists in the strong conviction that a blank collection of good precepts will never change men's lives without an appeal to their feelings and their imaginations; but the ultimate end of his labours is to save his countrymen, to use his own dialect, from the clutches of the devil, and, in any case, from the tyranny of vice and selfishness."—(Leslie Stephen, vol. ii. p. 411.)

"To Whitefield may be traced the revival, so far as the Church of England is concerned. It is true that he himself practically became a Dissenter, and that to his labours the formation of the Countess of Huntingdon's Connexion may mainly be attributed; and it is true also that there was in him much less of the Churchman, less reverence for tradition and precedents, as well as less disposition to put trust in sacraments, than in his great coadjutor, Wesley. When the latter founded the great Society which bears his name, he necessarily drew off from the Established Church his immediate disciples. But Whitefield always maintained an intimate friendship with the best of the clergy, and they acknowledged their indebtedness to him. Newton was his convert, and Venn was not only his friend, but had such profound respect for him that he did not hesitate to offend the prejudices of his order by preaching in the Tabernacle the funeral sermon of one who had virtually become a Dissenter, who was, in fact, the most powerful Dissenter of his day."—(Rogers, p. 130.)

"The Evangelical school in the Church of England is clearly to be traced to Methodism." As Mr. Rogers truly says: "Not till Wesley and Whitefield arose, to be followed by Newton, Venn Scott, and Milner, and still later by Simeon and others, was there an Evangelical school."—(*Ibid.* p. 135.)

"The Anglican Church, which was rapidly decaying under the influence of Erastian dignitaries, was saved by the intense faith, the impassioned zeal, and the devoted labours of a few humble clergymen, whose names are redeemed from obscurity by the service they rendered to this great movement. They brought to it nothing but great spiritual qualities, and these were made mighty of God."—(*Ibid.* p. 132.)

"The effects of Whitefield's labours on succeeding times have been thrown into the shade by the more brilliant fortunes of the Ecclesiastical Dynasty of which Wesley was at once the founder, the lawgiver, and the head. Yet a large proportion of the American Churches, and that great body of the Church of England, which, assuming the title of 'Evangelical,' has been refused that of 'Orthodox,' may trace back their spiritual genealogy by regular descent from him. . . . The quarterings of Whitefield are entitled to a conspicuous place in the 'Evangelical' scutcheon;' and they who bear it are not wise in being ashamed of the blazonry. If the section of the Church of England which usually bears that title be properly so distinguished, there can be no impropriety in designating as her four evangelists John Newton

Thomas Scott, Joseph Milner, and Henry Venn."—(*Essays in Ecclesiastical Biography*, by the Right Hon. Sir James Stephen, K.C.B., p. 400.)

"On the other hand, the coincidence with the spirit and the doctrines of the Methodists, and especially of Whitefield, was such as to forbid the belief that there existed no other relations between the two bodies but that of a simultaneous existence. It has already, indeed, been shown that Newton was the disciple of Whitefield, that Scott[1] was the disciple of Newton, and that Milner was his imitator; and it would be easy to show that Venn lived in a long and friendly intercourse with the great itinerant, and officiated with him in places of public worship which rejected episcopal control."

"They were the sons, by natural or spiritual birth, of men who, in the earlier days of Methodism, had shaken off the lethargy in which, till then, the Church of England had been entranced—of men, by whose agency the great evangelic doctrine of faith, emerging in its primeval splendour, had not only overpowered the contrary heresies, but had perhaps obscured some kindred truths."—(*Essays in Ecclesiastical Biography*, by the Right Hon. Sir James Stephen, K.C.B.)

"Methodism is the third epoch-making phenomenon in the history of the Reformed Church of England. . . . It sought to quicken the State Church afresh, to introduce the principle of the Reformation as a sanctifying force into the life, and especially to bring the leaven of the gospel thoroughly to bear upon the mass of the people, which had been entirely neglected before. . . . From this despised Methodist Club (at Oxford) came the regeneration of the English Church, just as half a century before from the *Collegia pietatis* sprang the revival of the German Church."—(C. Schoell, in Herzog's *Real-Encyklopädie*, vol. ix. p. 681.)

"Before the close of the century the evangelical movement had become dominant in England, and it continued the almost undisputed centre of religious life till the rise of the Tractarian movement of 1830. But, beyond all other men, it was John Wesley to whom this work was due."—(Lecky, vol. ii. p. 627.)

"The influence of the movement transformed for a time the whole spirit of the Established Church, and has been more or less felt in every Protestant community speaking the English tongue." —(*Ibid.* p. 632.)

---

[1] "The writer who made a deeper impression on my mind than any other, and to whom, humanly speaking, I almost owe my soul—Thomas Scott, of Aston Sandford." References are made also to the powerful influence upon his mind of "a work of Romaine's;" to Law's *Serious Call;* and Milner's *Church History.*—(*Apologia pro Vita sua*, Cardinal Newman, pp. 5-7.)

"John Wesley, founder of the Methodist denomination, is one of the most blessed and renowned preachers of the Church of Christ since the Reformation. He is among the very foremost of the great and influential spirits of the eighteenth century. To him it was granted, by God's favour, to arouse the English Church, when it was ruined by a frigid deism, which lost sight of Christ the Redeemer, and was almost dead, to a renewed Christian life. By preaching the justifying and renewing of the soul through belief upon Christ, he lifted many thousands of the humbler classes of the English people from their exceeding ignorance and evil habits, and made them earnest, faithful Christians. His untiring effort made itself felt not in England alone, but in America and in Continental Europe. Not only the germs of almost all the existing zeal in England on behalf of Christian truth and life are due to Methodism, but the activity stirred up in other portions of Protestant Europe we must trace indirectly, at least, to Wesley."—(P. 516.)

"Wesley was the bishop of such a diocese as neither the Eastern nor the Western Church ever witnessed before. What is there in the circle of Christian effort—foreign missions, home missions, Christian tracts and literature, field-preaching, Circuit-preaching, Bible-readings, or aught else that may be named—which was not attempted by John Wesley, which was not grasped by his mighty mind through the aid of his Divine Leader?"—(Dr. K. H. Sack, Bonn, in *Leaders of the Church Universal*, p. 525. Dr. F. Piper, Berlin.)

"When Christianity was thus growing faint amidst general corruption, help came to it not from human wisdom or contrivance, not from the wisdom of Church or State, not from learning or intellectual power or philosophy, but from the meanest, the most humble, the most obscure sources. It was not the bishops and learned men who were enabled to turn the tide, though they strove manfully. It was the despised and obscure preachers of the gospel. By 'foolishness' the world was saved.

"A second movement, like that of Wycliffe, broke forth from the University of Oxford. Three young men arose, the two Wesleys and Whitefield—without station—graduates or undergraduates— and began the work of evangelization. They began by preaching in the prisons; they preached the gospel of repentance for the remission of sins—a change of heart. They went forth, without learning, to awaken their brethren slumbering in trespasses and sins—the virgins sleeping at their posts. Not by wisdom but by the foolishness of preaching, like the apostles, they won the world. Their work was irregular, beyond all common rules. They preached no profound doctrines gathered by man's ingenuity out of the Scriptures—no philosophy, with its endless theories and vain illusions and contradictory conclusions—but simply repentance from dead works, and conversion to the living God—conversion to Him who completed the work of man's redemption on Calvary. Their forms of expression were sometimes rude or inaccurate, but their meaning in general was to recall a dead or dying world to the first principle of its religion, salvation through Christ—conversion with all the heart to God. And hence the marvellous and magnificent success which attended their work, hence the heaven-descended power which caused the human heart, even of the very least and most illiterate, to respond to the call of Heaven, to turn with bitter tears from its iniquities, and place itself under the dominion of the Most High. In comparison of such a work, which was national, and from whose influence no class or order of men was exempt, what are the minor points in which human infirmity may have shown itself in that direction? We can forgive everything—even Wesley's and Whitefield's mistakes—for the sake of the fervent testimony they bore to Christ, and to the cardinal doctrines of the gospel which they unceasingly preached.

"It was from this great movement that a reflex action passed over the whole Church of England. A part, indeed, of those who had been converted fell for a time into separation (one of those evils which we have to lament, and by which Satan has often contrived to render imperfect or to mar the greatest works of believers).

"But the effect on the whole Church of England was revivifying. Hence the stimulus applied to such men as Romaine, Cadogan, Newton, Cowper, Scott, Bickersteth, Martyn, Wilberforce— especially to the last, who, in his 'Practical View,' set before all classes, rich and poor, their paramount duties to Christianity, and the exalted hopes and promises on which these duties rested; and all strove together with one mind to glorify God in Christ; all fervently believed and faithfully preached the grand essential doctrines of revealed truth handed down from the beginning in the apostolic baptismal creeds."—(*A Narrative of Events connected with the Publication of the Tracts for the Times*, by William Palmer, pp. 10, 11.)

"It was from Britain that this grand Christian movement— the great work of the nineteenth century, the supplement of Wesley's great revival—arose. That bold, aggressive movement once more made Christianity the teacher of the world—silent, indeed, but not less effectual. It was, as it were, another Pentecost, another preaching of the gospel in all lands, even amongst its foes, a banner displayed in the face of an unbelieving world, an uplifting of the cardinal truths of the faith, a bold testimony, patent to all men, that the human race still clung to the worship of the Creator and Saviour.

"For the movement at once spread to all countries. It was hailed even in distant Russia. It was received with transports of joy by believers in all countries, even by all that was best and most Christian in the Roman priesthood. All joined in acknowledging, by their association with the Bible Society, the paramount claims, the undoubted authority of revealed truth.

"This was the grand result brought about by God's preservation of His own cause in Britain. The whole world became its debtor. Britain stood at the head of Christian nations. God had made it His great witness upon earth in the latter days."—(Palmer, p. 17.)

"But Methodism carried preaching out of consecrated buildings into private houses, public halls, city streets, and village greens. It gave a new impetus to prayer-meetings on week-days; it led to gatherings for religious conversation. Classes and love-feasts were not adopted by the old Dissent any more than by the orthodox Church; but a tendency to social spiritual engagements, beyond those of the stereotyped order, was, doubtless, one of the effects produced by the Methodist revival."—(Stoughton, vol. vi. p. 429.)

"Methodism was already a great spiritual power in the country. Not sixty years old in its full organization, it exerted an influence far beyond its own borders, and, as seen in the light of history since, it carried within an inspiration which awakened men's souls to a sense of religion all over the world." . . . "The effects of Methodism were felt outside itself; they penetrated the Church of England and Dissenting denominations."—(Stoughton, vol. vii. pp. xxii. xxiii.)

"A new race had risen up. Religious revivalists, if not ecclesiastical reformers, were on the increase, and coming to the front. Methodism was infusing its spirit into the minds of men who dwelt outside its borders."—(Stoughton, vol. vi. p. 443.)

"Quakers, like other religionists, came in contact with Methodism. The great revival undoubtedly influenced the Society, but not to any very large extent. Wesley seems hardly to have moved them as much as Whitefield. Whitefield had more sympathy with them, for he dwelt on the hidden life of the soul— 'a light which never was on sea or shore '—' Christ in the heart, the secret of spiritual-mindedness.' "—(Stoughton, vol. vi. p. 390.)

"The revival of evangelical religion, popular preaching, Sunday schools, and new religious societies, were immense gains. They not only produced immediate effects conspicuous on the surface, but they penetrated efficaciously into the depths of society, so as to render the continuance of certain existing evils almost impossible."—(Stoughton, vol. vi. p. 446.)

"I have often heard my father speak of Wesley. It was always in the mode represented by an answer he once gave me to the question, 'How do you account for the fact that England, at the end of the eighteenth century, escaped a revolution like that of France?' 'O,' he said at once, 'there is not the least doubt as to that: England escaped a political revolution because she had undergone a religious revolution.' 'You mean that brought about by Wesley and Whitefield?' 'Of course!'"— (*Life of Maurice*.)

"A revival broke out which changed in a few years the whole temper of English society. . . . Religion carried to the hearts of the poor a fresh spirit of moral zeal, while it purified our literature and our manners. A new philanthropy reformed our prisons, infused clemency and wisdom into our penal laws, abolished the slave trade, and gave the first impulse to popular education. Charles Wesley came to add sweetness to this sudden, startling light. . . . . A new musical impulse was aroused in the people, which gradually changed the face of public devotion throughout England."—(J. R. Green, p. 718.)

E. PAGE 163.

"Methodism includes a group of Societies, all of which have the same characteristics, and in the main hold by the same principles, and work on the same plans. The theology of all is marked by evangelical simplicity; they alike preach with fervour and directness a message of salvation addressed to humanity at large; they have the same general principles of polity, and they all trust largely to the influence of social Christianity in the meeting for fellowship as an important instrument for consolidation and extension. The work of all must be taken into account when any attempt is made to estimate the extent of the dominion over which the influence of Methodism reaches, or to appraise the service which it is rendering to Christianity.

"The story of its progress is little less than a romance. Little more than a century ago its first Conference was held, and to-day it counts its adherents by millions; it has its settlements in every part of the world; it is universally recognised as one of the most potent religious forces, not only in this country, but in that Greater Britain which is peopled by the English race and dominated by English ideas."—(Rogers, p. 550.)

THE FERNLEY LECTURES.

The Holy Spirit: His Work and Mission. By G. OSBORN, D.D. Demy 8vo, paper covers, 6d.

The Person of Christ: Dogmatic, Scriptural, Historical. With Two additional Essays on the Biblical and Ecclesiastical Development of the Doctrine, and Illustrative Notes. By the Rev. W. B. POPE, D.D. Demy 8vo, cloth, 7s.

Jesus Christ, the Propitiation for our Sins. By the Rev. JOHN LOMAS. Demy 8vo, sewed, price 6d.

The Holy Catholic Church, the Communion of Saints. With Notes and Essays on the History of Christian Fellowship, and on the Origin of 'High Church' and 'Broad Church' Theories. By the Rev. BENJAMIN GREGORY, D.D. Demy 8vo, 290 pages, paper covers, 3s. 6d.; cloth, 4s. 6d.

The Doctrine of a Future Life as contained in the Old Testament Scriptures. By the Rev. JOHN DURY GEDEN. Second Edition. Demy 8vo, paper covers, 1s.; cloth, 2s.

The Priesthood of Christ. With Notes by the Rev. HENRY W. WILLIAMS, D.D. Demy 8vo, paper covers, 1s.; cloth, 2s.

Modern Atheism: Its Position and Promise. By the Rev. EBENEZER E. JENKINS, M.A. Demy 8vo, paper covers, 1s.; cloth, 2s.

Life and Death, the Sanctions of the Law of Love. By G. W. OLVER, B.A. (Published for the Author.) Demy 8vo, sewed, 1s.; cloth, 2s.

Life, Light, and Love: The Principles of Holiness. By ALFRED J. FRENCH, B.A. Demy 8vo, paper covers, 1s.; cloth, 2s.

Christianity and the Science of Religion. By the Rev. JOHN SHAW BANKS. Demy 8vo, paper covers, 1s.; cloth, 2s.

The Dogmatic Principle in relation to Christian Belief. By the Rev. F. W. MACDONALD. Demy 8vo, paper covers, 1s.; cloth, 2s.

The Witness of the Spirit. By the Rev. ROBERT NEWTON YOUNG, D.D. Demy 8vo, paper covers, 1s.; cloth, 2s.

On the Difference between Physical and Moral Law. By the Rev. WILLIAM ARTHUR, M.A. Demy 8vo, paper covers, 2s.; cloth, 3s.

The Universal Mission of the Church of Christ. By the Rev. B. HELLIER. Demy 8vo, paper covers, 1s.; cloth, 2s.

Methodism in the Light of the Early Church. By the Rev. W. F. SLATER, M.A. Demy 8vo, paper covers, 1s. 6d.; cloth, 2s. 6d.

The Influence of Scepticism on Character. By the Rev. W. L. WATKINSON. Demy 8vo, paper covers, 1s. 6d.; cloth, 2s. 6d.

The Creator, and what we may know of the Method of Creation. By the Rev. W. H. DALLINGER, LL.D., F.R.S. Demy 8vo, paper covers, 1s. 6d.; cloth, 2s. 6d.

The Christian Conscience. A Contribution to Christian Ethics. By Rev. W. T. DAVISON, M.A. Demy 8vo, paper covers, 2s.; cloth, 3s.

The Credentials of the Gospel: A Statement of the Reason of the Christian Hope. Fourth Thousand. By Rev. JOSEPH AGAR BEET. Demy 8vo, paper covers, 1s. 6d.; cloth, 2s. 6d.

LONDON: WESLEYAN METHODIST BOOK-ROOM,
2, CASTLE STREET, CITY ROAD, E.C.; AND 66, PATERNOSTER ROW, E.C.

RECENT FERNLEY LECTURES.

The Credentials of the Gospel: A Statement of the Reason of the Christian Hope. Being the Fernley Lecture for 1889. By Rev. JOSEPH AGAR BEET. Fourth Thousand. Demy 8vo, paper covers, 1s. 6d. ; cloth, gilt lettered, 2s. 6d.

'An uncommonly interesting production. The matter is digested with admirable skill, and the expression is clear as Horace's "Bandusian Spring," and precise as logic itself.'—*The Christian World.*

'Emphatically a good book, clear and compact in its statements, logical and incisive in its reasoning, and pungent in its appeals. . . . The work of a thinker as well as a scholar.'—*British Weekly.*

'However well read in apologetic literature any one is, he will find much to interest and much to convince in the chapters which deal with the resurrection and the miraculous. At this point Prof. Beet makes a distinct advance in the argument, and deserves the thanks of all who are interested in the defence of Christianity. The book is throughout written in an admirable style.'—Dr. MARCUS DODS in the *Expositor.*

The Christian Conscience: A Contribution to Christian Ethics. Being the Fernley Lecture for 1888. By Rev. W. T. DAVISON, M.A. Demy 8vo, paper covers, 2s. ; cloth, 3s.

'Acute, forcible, and interesting. . . . Treats a large subject entirely without superficiality, and yet in a popular style.'—*Scotsman.*

'Unquestionably one of the finest and most timely deliverances that has ever emanated from the Fernley chair.'—*Lincolnshire Free Press.*

The Creator, and what we may know of the Method of Creation. By the Rev. W. H. DALLINGER, D.D., LL.D., F.R.S. Ninth Thousand. Paper covers, 1s. 6d. ; cloth, 2s. 6d.

'A most carefully written discourse, and will unquestionably be read with profit by the thoughtful reader.'—*Scientific Enquirer.*

'Contains as much real thought, sound philosophy, logical reasoning, and solid instruction as are found only in large treatises.'—*Oldham Chronicle.*

'It would be difficult to name another book in which the relations of religion and science are so ably treated.'—*Sunday School Chronicle.*

The Influence of Scepticism on Character. By the Rev. W. L. WATKINSON. Seventh Thousand. 8vo, paper covers, 1s. 6d. ; cloth, 2s. 6d.

'Demonstrates very ably and clearly the demoralizing effects of scepticism.'—*The Record.*

'Outspoken and ably written.'—*Leeds Mercury.*

'It enters very thoroughly into the subject, and numerous examples are given of the deteriorating effect of unbelief in the human character.'—*Daily Chronicle.*

'The book is one of remarkable vigour.'—*Christian.*

'No subject could be more timely . . . none more suited to his genius.'—*Wesleyan Methodist Magazine.*

'Sees his position with clearness, and defends it with enthusiastic force.'—*Saturday Review.*

'Thoughtful, incisive, and full of a practical view and estimate of infidelity.'—*Liverpool Mercury.*

LONDON: WESLEYAN METHODIST BOOK-ROOM,
2, CASTLE STREET, CITY ROAD, E.C. ; AND 66, PATERNOSTER ROW, E.C.

Methodism in the Light of the Early Church. By the Rev. W. F. SLATER, M.A. 8vo, paper covers, 1s. 6d.; cloth, gilt lettered, 2s. 6d.

'Very learned and very popular . . . the result of wide and well-digested reading, and of clear, strong, original thought.'—*Wesleyan Methodist Magazine.*

'A very important and interesting contribution to Church History . . . is worthy to rank with any of the previous fourteen.'—*Christian World Pulpit.*

'This lecture is written with a fulness of knowledge and a breadth of spirit that proclaim the scholarship and piety of its author.'—*Hastings and St. Leonard's Chronicle.*

On the Difference between Physical and Moral Law. By WILLIAM ARTHUR. Sixth Thousand. Demy 8vo, paper covers, 2s.; cloth, 3s.

'It is the most masterly and triumphant refutation of the modern atheistic hypothesis . . . which we have met for many a day.'—*Expositor.*

'A singularly able and thoughtful book.'—*Church of England Quarterly.*

'A suggestive book, full of eloquent passages and pregnant remarks.'—*The Spectator.*

'It deals with some of the deepest problems presented both by physical and metaphysical science, and it deals with them with a master-hand.'—*The Congregationalist.*

'We have rarely perused an equally clear and perspicuous piece of reasoning.'—*Contemporary Review.*

THE FERNLEY LECTURES, Volume I.
8vo, cloth, 12s. CONTENTS:—

The Holy Spirit: His Work and Mission. By GEORGE OSBORN, D.D.
The Person of Christ: Dogmatic, Scriptural, Historical. By Rev. W. B. POPE, D.D.
Jesus Christ, the Propitiation for our Sins. By Rev. JOHN LOMAS.
The Holy Catholic Church, the Communion of Saints. By BENJAMIN GREGORY, D.D.

THE FERNLEY LECTURES, Volume II.
Demy 8vo, cloth, 12s. CONTENTS:—

The Doctrine of a Future Life as contained in the Old Testament Scripture. By Rev. JOHN DURY GEDEN.
The Priesthood of Christ. By Rev. H. W. WILLIAMS, D.D.
Modern Atheism: Its Position and Promise. By Rev. EBENEZER E. JENKINS, M.A.
Life, Light, and Love: The Principles of Holiness. By Rev. ALFRED J. FRENCH, B.A.
Christianity and the Science of Religion. By Rev. J. SHAW BANKS.
The Dogmatic Principles in relation to Christian Belief. By Rev. W. F. MACDONALD.
The Witness of the Spirit. By Rev. ROBERT NEWTON YOUNG, D.D.
On the Difference between Physical and Moral Law. By Rev. WILLIAM ARTHUR, M.A.

THE FERNLEY LECTURES, Volume III.
Demy 8vo, cloth, 12s. CONTENTS:—

The Universal Mission of the Church of Christ. By Rev. B. HELLIER.
Methodism in the Light of the Early Church. By Rev. W. F. SLATER, M.A.
The Influence of Scepticism on Character. By Rev. W. L. WATKINSON.
The Creator, and what we may know of the Method of Creation. By Dr. DALLINGER.
The Christian Conscience. A Contribution to Christian Ethics. By Rev. W. T. DAVISON, M.A.

LONDON: WESLEYAN METHODIST BOOK-ROOM,
2, CASTLE STREET, CITY ROAD, E.C.; AND 66, PATERNOSTER ROW, E.C.

BY THE REV. BENJAMIN GREGORY, D.D.

Consecrated Culture: Memorials of Benjamin Alfred Gregory, M.A. Crown 8vo, with Portrait, 5s.

'Of singular beauty and instructiveness. . . . It passes out of the region of mere biography, and is a contribution to the social and religious history of our times.'—*Monthly Review.*

Sermons, Addresses, and Pastoral Letters. Demy 8vo, with Portrait of the Author, 5s.

'Fresh, strong, and pungent,—all alive with the yearnings of an urgent spirit, and lit up by penetrating remarks and happy allusions and quotations.'—*British Quarterly Review.*

The Holy Catholic Church, the Communion of Saints. Being the Fernley Lecture for 1873. With Notes and Essays on the History of Christian Fellowship, and on the Origin of 'High Church' and 'Broad Church' Theories. Demy 8vo, 290 pp., 4s. 6d.

'We could not name a more admirable and satisfactory dissertation on the subject, or one more deserving of careful study and reflection.' *Irish Evangelist.*

The Thorough Business Man. Memoirs of Walter Powell, Merchant, London and Melbourne. Seventh Edition. Crown 8vo, with Portrait, 3s. 6d.

'Unique as a *vade mecum* for young men. Its principles, if acted upon as Walter Powell acted upon them, would not only be the best guarantee of commercial success, but would exalt commercial life to a religious power as great as that of the pulpit.' *British Quarterly Review.*

BY THE REV. W. B. POPE, D.D.

A Compendium of Christian Theology. Being Analytical Outlines of a Course of Theological Study, Biblical, Dogmatic, Historical. Three Vols. Demy 8vo, cloth, £1, 2s. 6d.; half morocco, cloth sides, £1, 11s.

A Higher Catechism of Theology. Crown 8vo, 5s.; half morocco, 8s.

The Inward Witness, and other Discourses. 8vo, 7s.

'Will prove a great blessing. . . . We heartily welcome the volume.' *Primitive Methodist World.*

'Resplendent with the light of living doctrine . . . the very soul of Scripture.' *Irish Christian Advocate.*

Discourses: Chiefly on the Lordship of the In-carnate Redeemer. Third and Enlarged Edition. Demy 8vo, 8s. 6d.

'They have a thorough groundwork of exegetical, doctrinal, and experimental knowledge, so that they are both full and ripe; and they are conspicuously evangelical.'—*British and Foreign Evangelical Review.*

Sermons, Addresses, and Charges. Delivered during his Year of Office. Published by Request. Demy 8vo, 8s. 6d.

The Prayers of St Paul. Being an Analysis and Exposition of the Devotional Portions of the Apostle's Writings. Demy 8vo, 7s.

The Person of Christ: Dogmatic, Scriptural, His-torical. The Fernley Lecture for 1871. With Two additional Essays on the Biblical and Ecclesiastical Development of the Doctrine, and Illustrative Notes. New and Enlarged Edition. Demy 8vo, 7s.

LONDON: WESLEYAN METHODIST BOOK-ROOM,
2, CASTLE STREET, CITY ROAD, E.C.; AND 66, PATERNOSTER ROW, E.C.

BY THE REV. J. SHAW BANKS.

Christianity and the Science of Religion. Demy 8vo, paper covers, 1s.; cloth, 2s.
'Marked by compression, incisiveness, and force.'—*The Watchman.*

Martin Luther, the Prophet of Germany. Fcap. 8vo. Thirteen Illustrations. 1s. 6d.
'For general use, we do not know of a better biography in so small a space.'—*Sword and Trowel.*

Our Indian Empire: Its Rise and Growth. Imperial 16mo. Thirty-five Illustrations and Map. 3s. 6d.
'A well-condensed and sensibly written popular narrative of Anglo-Indian History.'—*Daily News.*

Three Indian Heroes: The Missionary; the Soldier; the Statesman. Numerous Illustrations. Small crown 8vo, 1s. 6d.

A Preacher's Library. Hints on Theological Reading. Second Edition. Demy 8vo, 8d.

A Preacher's General Reading: Companion to 'A Preacher's Library.' Demy 8vo, 6d.

BY THE REV. W. L. WATKINSON.

The Influence of Scepticism on Character. Seventh Thousand. 8vo, paper covers, 1s. 6d.; cloth, 2s. 6d.
'Demonstrates very ably and clearly the demoralizing effects of scepticism.'—*The Record.*
'Outspoken and ably written.'—*Leeds Mercury.*

Noonday Addresses delivered in the Central Hall, Manchester. Crown 8vo, stiff covers, 1s.; cloth, gilt lettered, 1s. 6d.
'He rebukes the specious sophisms of high-churchism and unbelief alike. He is moreover a master of the English tongue, and is rich in imagery and illustration.'—*Wesleyan Methodist Magazine.*

The Lessons of Prosperity; and other Addresses delivered at Noonday in the Philosophical Hall, Leeds. Crown 8vo, stiff covers, 1s.; cloth, gilt lettered, 1s. 6d.
'Present that combination of philosophical acuteness, keen analysis of character, apt illustration, accurate expression, and practical wisdom generally found in what he writes.'—*Leeds Mercury.*

Mistaken Signs; and other Papers on Christian Life and Experience. Fourth Thousand. Crown 8vo, stiff covers, 1s.; cloth, gilt lettered, 1s. 6d.
'His comparisons are charming, his statements are clear, his convictions are strong, and his whole work goes to nourish an honest, healthy, heavenly inner life.'—*Sword and Trowel.*

Life of John Wicklif. Crown 8vo, with Portrait engraved on Steel, and Eleven whole-page Illustrations, 2s. 6d.
'The best popular sketch we have seen of the life, labours, and writings of the great Reformer.'—*Daily Chronicle.*
'Carefully planned. . . . All essential facts are here.'—*Literary World.*

LONDON: WESLEYAN METHODIST BOOK-ROOM,
2, CASTLE STREET, CITY ROAD, E.C.; AND 66, PATERNOSTER ROW, E.C.

NEW AND RECENT BOOKS.

'A Piece of an Honeycomb.' Meditations for Every Day in the Year. Crown 8vo. Red lines round each page. Cloth, red edges, 4s.

'An exquisite volume in every respect. It is no mere collection of commonplace reflections on various texts, but a rich storehouse of beautifully short and practically helpful thoughts of just the kind that intelligent and earnest Christians need for daily refreshment and guidance. . . . Our readers should by all means secure the book for themselves, and for any friends in whom they are interested.'—*Wesleyan Methodist Magazine*.

By Canoe and Dog-Train among the Cree and Salteaux Indians. By the Rev. EGERTON RYERSON YOUNG. Introduction by Rev. MARK GUY PEARSE. With Photographic Portraits of Rev. E. R. YOUNG, Map, and Thirty-two Illustrations. Sixth Thousand. Imperial 16mo, 3s. 6d.

'As we turn page after page of this book, we meet with crisp and even humorous incidents, thrilling escapes, privations patiently borne, graphic sketches of native life and character, and, best of all, evidences on all hands of the power of the gospel of the Lord Jesus Christ.'—*Illustrated Missionary News*.

Rambles and Reveries of a Naturalist. By REV. WILLIAM SPIERS, M.A., F.G.S., F.R.M.S. etc., Co-Editor of the *Journal of Microscopy and Natural Science*. Large crown 8vo, with more than Sixty Illustrations, 2s. 6d.

'Mr. Spiers is accurate, painstaking, and practical. . . . He writes as one who knows his subject—soberly, reasonably, and attractively.'—*Methodist Recorder*.

The Sabbath for Man : An Inquiry into the Origin and History of the Sabbath Institution. With a Consideration of its Claims upon the Christian, the Church, and the Nation. By Rev. WILLIAM SPIERS, M.A., F.G.S., F.R.M.S., etc. Large crown 8vo, 2s. 6d.

'We commend this book very highly as an able exposition and successful defence of orthodox teaching on the Christian Sabbath.'—*Methodist New Connexion Magazine*.

Among the Pimento Groves : A Story of Negro Life in Jamaica. By Rev. HENRY BUNTING. Six full-page Illustrations. Crown 8vo, 2s.

'A charmingly written account of the introduction and spread of Christianity among the West Indian Negroes. It should be in every Sunday-school library in the country.'—*King's Highway*.

The Happy Valley: Our New 'Mission Garden' in Uva, Ceylon. By Rev. S. LANGDON. Crown 8vo, with Map, Portrait of Mrs. WISEMAN, and numerous Illustrations, 2s.

Short Talks for the Times. By MARK GUY PEARSE. Seventh Thousand. Small crown 8vo, 1s. 6d.

Wesley his own Biographer. Being Selections from the Journals of Rev. JOHN WESLEY, A.M. To be completed in about Ten Sixpenny Monthly Parts. With numerous Illustrations. Part I., 64 pp., crown 4to, 6d. Now ready. To be completed in Eleven Parts.

LONDON : WESLEYAN METHODIST BOOK-ROOM,
2, CASTLE STREET, CITY ROAD. E.C. ; AND 66, PATERNOSTER ROW, E.C.